WHAT PEOPLE ARE SAYING ABOUT

A WOMAN'S WORTH

This important 21st century re-examination of that most perennial of wisdom texts the Bible does something you thought couldn't be done – it unearths fresh insights and offers them up with humor, grace and urgency.

Many have written about the harm done by the Bible and by those who would speak for it, but few have written so clearly and accessibly about the liberating humanism and therapeutic power conveyed by the ancient stories of the women of the Bible.

A spiritual teacher, astrologer, comic, novelist, and above all conjurer, Maggy Whitehouse brings clear eyes, deep thought and a loving heart to the mysterious process of unlocking wisdom from its ancient vaults. Let this book entertain you, embolden you and awaken you to the power of your own essential nature. Thank you, Maggy Whitehouse, for a good read, a slap in the face and a warm cup of tea by the fire. Good Lord, woman, you know how to call up Truth and Beauty with the stroke of a keyboard.

Peter Bolland, Professor of Humanities and Philosophy, Southwestern College, San Diego.

In the last thirty years or so there have been many books about the women who appear in the Bible, but never one like this.

Maggy Whitehouse reads the texts as a Kabbalist, which must have been nearer to the way biblical texts were read in the time of Jesus than many recent approaches. Modern fashions in scholarship have brought us literary criticism, rhetorical criticism, and above all the scepticism that is born of an over-literal reading of ancient texts. Philo, however, a highly educated Jew in Egypt in the mid-first century CE, would have recognised Maggy Whitehouse's approach to the Hebrew Bible. She enables her readers to look at the women of ancient Israel in the way the first Christians would have known them.

This is a fascinating book.

Dr. Margaret Barker, author of *The Hidden Tradition of the Kingdom of God* and *The Lady in the Temple* (T&T Clark).

This is a most scholarly and insightful exercise. It brings the attention to review the usually unconsidered side of the feminine as regards the different levels of the Bible and its folklore. Much food for thought.

Z'ev ben Shimon Halevi, author of *A Kabbalistic View of History* (Kabbalah Society).

A Woman's Worth

The Divine Feminine in the
Hebrew Bible

A Woman's Worth

The Divine Feminine in the Hebrew Bible

Maggy Whitehouse

AXIS MUNDI
BOOKS

Winchester, UK
Washington, USA

First published by Axis Mundi Books, 2013
Axis Mundi Books is an imprint of John Hunt Publishing Ltd., Laurel House, Station Approach,
Alresford, Hants, SO24 9JH, UK
office1@jhpbooks.net
www.johnhuntpublishing.com
www.axismundi-books.com

For distributor details and how to order please visit the 'Ordering' section on our website.

Text copyright: Maggy Whitehouse 2013

ISBN: 978 1 78099 834 3

A CIP catalogue record for this book is available from the British Library.

Design: Lee Nash

Printed and bound by CPI Group (UK) Ltd, Croydon, CR0 4YY

We operate a distinctive and ethical publishing philosophy in all
areas of our business, from our global network of authors to
production and worldwide distribution.

CONTENTS

Introduction

There is a woman's heart at the heart of God.
– Hebridean saying

Sometimes when you want to describe something, you first have to explain what it is not.

This is not a book by a scholar although it is indebted to the work of many academics, teachers and researchers. Neither is it a book by a feminist who wants to justify the actions of all the women in the Bible and demonize the men. It is more a journalistic attempt to provide a modern, metaphysical commentary on the stories of the women in the Hebrew Bible.

It is a series of psychological and spiritual portraits that came out of my own searching for the Divine Feminine within the Judaic mystical tradition known as Kabbalah.

Several traditions, including the seminal kabbalistic text the *Zohar*, place Adam, Eve, Abraham, Isaac and Jacob, Moses, Aaron, Joseph and David onto the kabbalistic Tree of Life, each one representing an aspect of the Holy One. The wives of the Patriarchs – Sarah, Rebekah, Leah and Rachel – are occasionally included but generally only in association with their husbands. But this is not the full story. The Matriarchs, together with many other women in the Hebrew Testament, also fit onto the Tree of Life in their own right, and placing them there gives their stories a new depth and relevance to us today.

The women's stories, told chronologically, tell of 'the fall' from Eden and then the rising back up the Tree of Life, from the base to the place of kingship, demonstrating growth from lives ruled by social convention into the actions of heroines who represent the Divine Feminine in the world. This chronology cannot be a coincidence; whether it was intended by the writers of the Hebrew Testament as part of the Hidden Tradition or whether it is through the Grace of God, we will never know. But it deserves to be marked, examined and, hopefully, celebrated.

The kabbalistic teaching used in this book is not that of the Kabbalah Center, neither is it that of the Lurianic Kabbalah of orthodox Jewry. It is based on the Toledano Tradition, a renaissance of the work of the 16th century Rabbi Moses Cordovero, the author of *The Palm Tree of Deborah*. Cordovero was a mystic who could combine vision with interpretations of the patterns within Hebrew letters and in the sacred writings, and he produced the first full integration of the previous differing schools in kabbalistic interpretation. Much of his teaching became hidden, after his death in 1570, with the rise of a new impulse led by the followers of his pupil, Isaac Luria. This newer teaching saw the world as broken at the point of creation and arose to be a comfort and inspiration to the Jewish nation reeling from the Inquisition and expulsion from the Iberian Peninsula. It had a powerful message of an external force of evil which explained why bad things happened to good people.

Cordovero, and all the kabbalistic mystics before him, saw creation as perfect with any and all misfortunes being the result of the misuse of human free will, including opposition to or misinterpretation of the will of God for our greater good.

Research indicates that Cordovero's tradition is the nearest we have to that which may have been studied in Biblical times and which based itself on the patterns within the sacred Menorah of the First Temple of the Hebrews and on the design of the Temple itself, as given in the *Book of Exodus*. These were updated into the diagram of the Tree of Life by the school of Isaac the Blind in the 11th century. The Cordoveran tradition itself, together with its great diagram of the design and flow of the Universe, Jacob's Ladder, was revitalized in the late 20th century by the Sephardic Jewish mystic Z'ev ben Shimon Halevi.

There are many books on Kabbalah which are complex and dense but, just as music is made beautiful or discordant by the rests between the notes, it is the hidden aspects behind written traditions which can transform the ancient texts from harsh or incomprehensible to something which can inspire and serve all who come to them, whatever their system of belief. This veiled tradition is the Wisdom Tradition. It is sometimes referred to as the feminine line. The masculine would be the exoteric, written down and often set in stone; the feminine being oral, esoteric and fluid enough to update with every generation.

The two aspects work together – just as they would have done in the first Temple of the Israelites before it fell into alleged corruption and was reformed before the Babylonian exile in the sixth century BCE. Modern scholarship indicates that this temple revered Yahweh and Asherah as the male and female attributes of the One High God and included grain, incense and wine as its offerings to these deities.[1]

Asherah was driven into exile and Yahweh became the face of the one God. But the Divine Feminine did not vanish; her story is woven throughout the Hebrew Testament in the lives of its women. Exoterically, these are historical documents – some more accurate than others. Esoterically, they provide us with spiritual guidelines for living and return us to the living Tree of Life – often depicted as the almond tree or sacred grove of Asherah in the Hebrew Testament.

Most religions follow the exoteric content of their teachings and, at that level, it is easy to judge the Biblical Testaments as being anti-women. We are told of Eve who brought the first sin to the world; Miriam who criticized Moses and was afflicted with leprosy in return; Leah 'the unloved' who tricked Jacob into marriage; Rebekah who lied to make her husband bless her favorite son rather than his; Mary Magdalene, who had seven devils driven out of her and who was unjustly labeled as a prostitute for centuries. Only to the Virgin Mary is attributed all virtue. Together with the Christian stories of saints such as St. Agnes, St. Agatha and St. Rose of Lima, you could easily assume that the only good woman is a dead virgin.

But the stories of the women in the Hebrew Testament have psychological, spiritual and divine messages for us too. Placing them on the kabbalistic Tree of Life shows the women growing up and taking power in a way that can be inspirational to today's mother, businesswoman or self-help expert. We can learn from the stories of Miriam whose life was a well of 'living water' for the exiles in the desert; from Ruth who was willing to leave her home and tribe and trust in the God of her mother-in-law, Naomi; from Deborah, revered by warriors and generals; and from Esther, the simple girl who became Queen of Persia and became willing to offer her life for her people.

There are yet more stories to be told but, in understanding how to read the Bible through mystical eyes, you can perhaps decide whether you would like to find and interpret those for yourself.

Unless otherwise indicated, the Biblical text used throughout the book is from the King James Bible.

Part One

The Power of the Story

Chapter One

The Written and Oral Traditions

Happy is the one who finds wisdom, and the person who obtains understanding. For the gain from her is better than the gain from silver, and her profit is better than gold. She is more precious than rubies: and all the things you can desire are not to be compared unto her. Long life is in her right hand; and in her left hand riches and honor. Her ways are ways of pleasantness, and all her paths are peace. She is a tree of life to those who lay hold of her: and happy is one that holds fast to her. The Lord by wisdom has founded the earth; by understanding has he established the heaven.
Proverbs 3:13–19, my translation

There are many traditional forms of interpretation of the Jewish Bible or *Tanukh*. The best known is probably *Talmud*, the most significant collection of what was the Jewish oral tradition interpreting the *Torah*, the first five books of the Bible. There are two Talmuds but the best known and most used is the Babylonian Talmud which was published around 500 CE after being compiled, over several centuries, as a response to the destruction of the Second Temple by the Romans in 70 CE. The Jewish nation had been dispersed and it was believed that it was vitally important to hold onto and standardize the traditional teaching to stop it being further diluted or misinterpreted.

Talmud comes in two forms: the *Mishnah*, which was the oral tradition written down, and the *Gemara*, a Rabbinical analysis of and commentary on the Mishnah. The *Midrash* is stories that elaborate on the Mishnah and Gemara and there is also *Aggadah*, a collection of folklore, stories and advice ranging from medical to business matters.

Midrash is a good cover term for all the above. It means

'story' or 'interpretation'. Every theory or thesis on this foundation text for Judaism and Christianity is a kind of Midrash and each one is a product of its times. The traditionally-honored *Midrashim* were all written before the 13th century CE. They don't all agree but they all have the same goal: to give a wider picture or to attempt to make sense of the stories in the Hebrew Testament. Often they strive to find virtue where there appears to be none, kindness where the text implies cruelty, and a depth and knowledge of the Divine on the part of the protagonists which the modern seeker in a more secular world may find challenging.

There are said to be four levels of Midrash: *peshat*, which looks at the literal meaning of the text; *remez*, the Hebrew for 'hints', which explains the allegory or the story behind the text; *derash*, from the Hebrew *darash*, 'to inquire' or 'to seek', which examines the comparative meaning – how this is relevant to us today both as individuals and as community – and *sod*, meaning 'secret' or 'mystery', which looks at the heart and soul of the Divine intention and the magic and mystery behind creation. As the word Kabbalah originates from *qabalah* (Hebrew QBLH), meaning 'receive', the two can be seen to be synonymous – the 'received, hidden tradition'.

Most of these texts have been unavailable to those who were not either scholars or Jews for centuries. When I first began to research this book fifteen years ago, I spent hours in the library at the Masorti Synagogue in Finchley, London. But the explosion of information on the Internet has made many writings which were only available to the orthodox Jew available to all and opened the doors to widely different interpretations.

The difficulty with writing down an oral tradition is that it ceases to update itself. One of the reasons that the spoken tradition is so important is that it can remain relevant to every generation. The fear that makes scholars write down oral religious teachings is justified – they believe that the spoken word will become misunderstood, misinterpreted, taken out of context and degraded. However, exactly the same can occur when they *are* written down because the interpretation, the language, the mindset and the style can and will become archaic.

There was a rash of feminist interpretation of the Bible in the late 20th century which was, again, of its time. Now it is another generation that can benefit from the amazing primal truths in this great religious text. This book takes the women's stories back to the roots and reinterprets them for the 21st century using a strong foundation of an ancient system that has stood the test of time since the days of the First Temple in Jerusalem. Kabbalah uses a clear structure, a matrix of the Universe, a diagram of creation made in the image of God. Keep to the structure and you can update the teaching without corrupting it. If the theory does not fit the structure, then it must be readdressed. It is not a perfect system; nothing is. However, it is a system with discipline, boundaries and sound common sense.

The Relevance of the Tree of Life and Jacob's Ladder
The kabbalistic Tree of Life (fig. 1) reflects ten aspects of God in ten *sefirot*, or spheres, connected by 22 paths; the same number as the letters in the Hebrew alphabet. These sefirot are attributes such as Mercy, Understanding, Judgment and Wisdom. They equate to the pantheon of Greek and Roman gods and to the visible planets of the solar system. The god-name *El*, for example, is placed at the *sefira* of Hesed which is associated with both the god and the planet Jupiter. Hesed's attributes are kingship, justice, loving-kindness and mercy.

It may be that this many-aspects-of-God-in-one approach was the best way for a monotheistic culture to absorb all the alternative gods who were worshipped in Biblical times. The first commandment states: "Thou shalt have no other gods before my face" (Exodus 20:3). It does not say that no other gods existed. Other gods certainly were worshipped. In the modern, secular world we also have gods such as money, fame or glamor.

The Bible says that the original Tree of Life was in the Garden of Eden and legend tells that when humanity left that sacred place they were given the *Book of Raziel*[2] to help them find the way back. The oral version of this book is said, by mystics, to be the teaching of the Tree of Life, which clearly sets out the levels of awareness within a human being and shows us how to climb from tribal consciousness to becoming the vessel to receive the Grace of God and to transmit this Grace to the world. The Tree was depicted in the First Temple by the seven-branched candelabrum known as the *menorah*.

The Tree of Life exists at four levels or Four Worlds: physical, psychological, spiritual and divine. These equate to the four courts of the Temple, said to be watched over by four heavenly beings, now known as the archangels Uriel, Gabriel, Raphael and Michael but, before the Babylonian exile, known as the Wonderful Counselor, the Mighty God, the Prince of Peace and the Heavenly Father.[3] Before the teachings of Isaac Luria became the norm for the study of Kabbalah, the Four Worlds were demonstrated in a structure known as *Jacob's Ladder*[4] (fig. 2).

The Divine World, known as *Azilut*, the Hebrew word for 'emanation' or 'calling forth', is the image of God, the perfected human being known as Adam Kadmon. Tradition tells us that this primordial human being is the dream of God – a perfect reflection of the Divine. All human souls originate here and descend through the lower Worlds to become independent and to learn, through free will, to return as perfected beings. When all humanity has completed that great journey, God will behold God and creation will be complete. In the feminine tradition this is told as God wishing to give birth to Itself in manifest reality. This World is associated with the element of Fire and is given the color of white or gold.

The second World, *Beriah*, Hebrew for Creation, is the realm of the archangels and concepts of creation. Here would be the Holy One's idea of a horse, rather than the existence of a horse – the pure essence of horse. This World is associated with the element of Air and is given the color of blue.

The third World, *Yezirah*, the Hebrew word for Formation, is where the idea becomes specific – what the horse looks like and how it moves. Is it a Haflinger rather than a Lipizzaner; a chestnut rather than a grey; a stallion rather than a mare? It is still an image rather than reality but it has a form. This World is associated with the element of Water and is given the color of purple.

The fourth World, *Asiyyah*, the Hebrew word for Action, is where the three higher Worlds become manifest in reality and the individual horse is born. This world is associated with the element of Earth and is given the color of red.

The Biblical source for this four-part structure comes from Isaiah 43:4: *"Every one that is called by my name: for I have created him for my glory, I have formed him; yea, I have made him."* These four levels are also represented in both Hebrew Temples. The Torah says that the Tabernacle must have *"curtains of fine twined linen, and blue, and purple, and scarlet"* (Exodus 26:1).

Each of the Worlds blends with the ones above or below it so that Fire melds with Air, Air melds with Water and Water melds with Earth. Each of the lower Worlds presents a slightly coarser aspect of the ten Divine attributes of Azilut which, in turn, is only a reflection of the whole of the glory of God, beyond existence, ineffable and transcending all thought.

Names of God

In kabbalistic tradition, Azilut contains the ten names of God which are used in the Hebrew Testament (fig. 3). There is debate about the placing of a few of the names on the sefirot but they are largely consistent. Two of these names have distinctly feminine aspects: *Elohim* and *El Shaddai*.

The ultimate name of God, as told to Moses at the Burning Bush, is *Eheyeh Asher Eheyeh*, 'I Will Be That Which I Will Be', generally translated as 'I Am That I Am'. This name is reflected in the four letters known as the Tetragrammaton, YHVH, which refers to the aspect of the Divine known as Yahweh or Jehovah. The literal Hebrew meaning of YHVH is 'He Is'. It can also be translated as 'He Who Is'. It is regarded as having the same meaning as Eheyeh Asher Eheyeh but it is always translated in the Hebrew Testament as 'the LORD' in capitals. Jews are forbidden to say or write this name and, when reading the Torah, pronounce it as *Adonai*.

However, in this book the word 'Lord' has been written in lower case so as to allow the equality between Yahweh and Elohim.

On the Tree of Life of Azilut, Yahweh and Elohim spring from the highest sefira of Eheyeh. They meet in the place known as *Tiferet*, the sefira of truth and beauty, as *Yahweh Elohim*, known kabbalistically as both the Holy One and the Creator. From Yahweh Elohim springs *El Hai Shaddai*, the Living Almighty/the Holy Spirit and from her, *Adonai*, the Lord and/or the *Shekhinah*, the presence of God (see Chapter Three). The Divine Light of God flows down the Tree, filling and then overflowing each sefira. Yahweh and Elohim come together in unison to give birth to Shaddaï and Adonai, making the Elohim both bride and mother of the Lord.

As Adonai is at the base sefira of Azilut, the Divine World, and this sefira is known as *Malkhut*, 'kingdom', Kabbalah teaches that Adonai is placed at 'the Kingdom of God'.

The Messiah is also placed here; the sefira being also the center point – the Tiferet – of Beriah and the top – Keter (crown) – of Yezirah. This means that he, or she, who rises to this position spiritually would have embraced the three upper Worlds and have all power over the physical World of Asiyyah. It would be perfectly possible for this person to resurrect a physical body.

When Jesus adjures us to reach for the Kingdom of God, he is telling us of the highest point of human consciousness where we are one with the Divine.

In Judaism, the Messiah has not yet come; in Christianity, he is Jesus Christ who will come again. However, in kabbalistic lore there is what might be called a 'lesser messiah' in every generation – an Anointed One who bears the mantle of God for each age of humanity. In the Hebrew Testament, these leaders come to save their people but the story is told as being primarily a physical salvation. This may be the reason why Jesus was expected to liberate the Jews from the Roman occupation of Judea. However, their stories can also be uplifting for our souls and spirits if read allegorically or metaphysically. Moses is believed to have been an Anointed One and so is King David. Queen Esther is said to be the first, known female Anointed One of God, the Divine Feminine on Earth.

Chapter Two

The Four Levels of the Bible

The Bible is said to be the most-read book in history even though, for most of that history, the majority of people in the world could not read or write. In New Testament times, even in Rome, 95 percent of the population was illiterate. It wasn't about whether they were smart or not: there was very little need to read – no novels, no biographies, no newspapers. Nearly everything that was written was about religion, politics, economics or contracts and would be read out loud by scribes to those who needed to know, or declared to the populace by town criers. When it came to stories, people would listen to a storyteller and repeat those stories themselves for family and friends.

Before the printing press, storytellers were the news presenters of the ages. They were listened to with the same avid fascination – a trait that continued well into the late 20th century in countries such as China. I remember being intrigued by a large crowd of people outside a restaurant in the northwestern city of Lanzhou in 1984. After several minutes of working my way through the crowd, I found that they weren't entranced by a fight or a floor show; it was the presence of an old lady telling a story at a table just outside the eating house. Everyone listening was silent, straining their ears. Some had their eyes closed for better concentration. They were people of all ages, from Mao-suited old men to young mothers with children.

With the possible exception of bedtime stories for children, the art of storytelling by individuals is dying out in the Western world. We have books and the Internet and movies for that purpose now. However, there is magic in a story that is passed on by word of mouth. It has time to update for every age, and they can be amended to bring in the children themselves or to become relevant to modern lives.

In our modern times of DVDs, movies and the Internet we have easy access to tens of millions of stories, many of which are violent, cruel or dedicated to warfare but woven within them are *still* the principles that underlie all myths: tales of good versus evil; of faith and courage; of the power of love and sacrifice; the presence of Grace – whether it is called God or not – and the continual message that eventually, one day, good will always win over evil.

It is said that these movies – and the books of today – carry just seven basic plots:[5]

Overcoming the Monster/the fight against evil
Rags to Riches
The Quest
Voyage and Return
Comedy
Tragedy
Rebirth

All seven plots have the same basic structure. For 'hero' here please read both genders – after all, 'Hero' is a woman's name from the Greek legend of Hero and Leander. Each plot starts with a character who has to face some kind of constriction or challenge.

- The Anticipation Stage (what the American mythologist Joseph Campbell terms the Call to Action) – the hero has to decide whether or not to take the challenge.
- The Dream Stage – all goes well for the hero.
- The Frustration Stage – the hero faces escalating conflict, usually in sets of three.
- The Nightmare Stage – all hope is lost.
- The Miraculous Escape.

This last stage varies, becoming one of the following:

- The hero triumphs against all odds (Overcoming the Monster).
- The bastard child turns out to be the legitimate heir of a huge fortune (Rags to Riches).
- The grail is found (The Quest).
- The hero returns from battle, gets the dream partner and they live happily ever after (Voyage and Return).
- All mistaken identities are sorted out or the protagonists pass their test and there is a marriage (Comedy).
- The hero, who has a fatal flaw, dies in the end or loses someone they love (Tragedy as in *Macbeth*).
- The hero dies, or appears to die, but is reborn stronger than ever (Rebirth – the story of Jesus in the Gospels of the New Testament... and nowadays the story of Harry Potter).

Aspects of all these stories and themes are redolent of the stories of the Bible women including the plot, if not the humor, of the comedy. Some of our heroines overcome the problems and some of them don't. Some, like Esther and Ruth, embrace several plots in one story and both experience rags to riches. Dinah experiences unrelieved tragedy. Jael and Deborah overcome the monster, Hannah finds the grail, Rachel and Leah experience tragedy and, through their husband Jacob, experience voyage and return. Rebekah and Sarah each demonstrate a fatal flaw and are faced with losing the ones they love.

What we have written down in the Bible is not necessarily the original teaching, nor necessarily an entirely representative version of the storytellers' tales. There is strong evidence that the Torah was edited in process, known as *tiqqûnê sôperîm*,[6] by what scholars call 'the Deuteronomists' both at the time, or after, the Babylonian exile (597 CE) when Judaism went through a transformation of the Temple and its teachings similar to the Catholic-to-

Protestant reformation in Europe in the sixteenth century CE.

Biblical Hebrew was a pictorial language without vowels. To give an English example of how it worked, the word SPHR could be read as *sphere, sapphire, suffer* and, even at a bit of a push, *supper* as well as the kabbalistic term *sefira*. The context would make it easier to understand but when every word in the sentence is open to interpretation you could find a whole wealth of possibilities – or give up in despair and rely on a scribe, a priest or a storyteller to explain.

The possibility of variations and interpretations is the most likely reason why the Hebrew Testament was set in stone, complete with added vowels, in what is known as the Masoretic text between the 7th and 10th centuries CE. This text does not vary much from an earlier text which was considered complete in the 2nd century but has some significant differences from the *Septuagint*, a Greek translation of the text which was made up to 400 years earlier.

However, the oral tradition continued, mostly in secret, generally within the orthodox community and rarely with the involvement of women.

Kabbalah and the Bible

Kabbalah is a structure, not a religion. It's a template; a blueprint; similar to the skeleton of a mammal. The basics are always the same, whether it is the skeleton of a mouse or a human being, but the apparatus that is attached to it and the way it is used can differ widely. It reveals patterns within the Biblical stories that correspond directly to the decorations and bowls on the Menorah in the Temple and the sefirot, *triads* or triangles and paths of the Tree of Life.

Because of those patterns, Kabbalists believe that the Bible can – and perhaps should – be read at four different levels in order for each story to become clear. The difference between Kabbalah and Mishnah is that Kabbalah holds to an existing set of guidelines and continually updates.

The first is the literal level: this story may or may not have happened. This relates to the physical World of Asiyyah.

Scholars, archaeologists and religious folk have a lot of fun with this level, as I did while researching this book. I really want the *Book of Ruth* to have been written before the *Book of Judges* in the Hebrew Testament so that all of my theories fit perfectly and Ruth's story takes place before Deborah's. In fact, most of the evidence indicates that the stories are contemporaneous and no one has any idea of the exact order in which they were written down. So we simply do not have a literal truth on the date for, or even on the existence of, the woman named Ruth or when her story was first told. We know in which order the stories are related in the Bible but that is all.

The second is the allegorical or moral level. This is the World of Yezirah.

This is about the meaning within the story. For most people, this is read as "obey God and you'll be all right – most of the time unless He's feeling quirky."

However, in the modern multicultural world where the law of cause and effect is more widely understood, we can see that the characters' behaviors draw specific consequences to them and we can learn from their choices or lack of decision.

For example, Jacob deceives his father, Isaac, to get the blessing of the older son and is, in turn, tricked by Laban, his cousin, into marrying the elder of his daughters instead of the younger whom he loves. So *what goes around comes around* is at the heart of this level of the teachings, although the lesson may take generations to be learnt.

The third is the metaphysical level. This is the World of Beriah.

At the metaphysical level, the stories are transpersonal. They may even be depictions of the Cosmic battle between good and evil. However, as each of the Worlds is interwoven with the others, Beriah and Yezirah are linked and the question of "what does this story have to say about my soul, my place in the Universe, my life's path and my spiritual quest?" is also important. This allows the Bible to be a path of learning for our collective consciousness. Often we can't see any sense from the microcosm but have to soar like an eagle to see the macrocosm.

Some Biblical stories will not be relevant to your life; others will hit a chord and others will be repellant. Ironically, it's often the ones that repel which are frequently the most important for us as they highlight subconscious issues we have with ourselves, with the world and with God that need to be resolved if we are to live happy and purposeful lives, and promote the spiritual development of humanity.

Biblical stories of atrocities, at this level of reading, refer not to real physical cruelty (though of course those may have happened) but to the aspects of our own inner psyche which are trying to destroy or degrade us or prevent our spiritual growth and which we, in turn, have to discipline or dissolve. To eradicate every one of an enemy army, in spiritual terms, means to clean up every aspect of our own lives so that the subconscious cannot destroy our hopes and dreams again. Just leaving one unhealthy aspect unexamined means that it can sneak up behind us again and again to our life's detriment.

The final level is the mystical. This is the World of Azilut.

The mystical level is about God's plan and the complete evolution of humanity as a whole. It is the place of the Divine within us and, in this book, it is about revealing the Divine Feminine within the women of the Hebrew Testament.

Incidentally, we are focusing on the *feminine* which exists within both men and women, as does the Sacred Masculine.

The Pillars of the Tree of Life

On the Tree of Life there are three vertical columns (fig. 1) The central column is known as the Column of Consciousness and is the main branch of the menorah. The two side pillars are represented as two olive trees as described in Zechariah's vision in the Hebrew Testament. The prophet is "woken as if out of sleep" by an angel who shows him the golden candlestick with bowls, pipes and lamps:

> *Then answered I, and said unto him, What are these two olive trees upon the right side of the candlestick and upon the left side thereof? And I answered again, and said unto him, What be these two olive branches which through the two golden pipes empty the golden oil out of themselves? And he answered me and said, Knowest thou not what these be? And I said, No, my lord.*
>
> *Then said he, These are the two anointed ones, that stand by the Lord of the whole earth.*
> Zechariah 4 11-14

The left-hand pillar represents the Elohim, the feminine or receptive attribute; the right-hand pillar, Yahweh the active, masculine attribute. They meet together as Yahweh Elohim on the central column (fig. 3). Some kabbalistic students have speculated, although not so far in print to my knowledge (often the problem with accreditation in an oral tradition), that any soul come to do great spiritual work in the world is partnered and supported by a soul-mate so that each can represent one pillar of the Tree of Life and find perfect balance by working together. This may or may not be a male-female partnership. St. Theresa and St. John of the Cross, Esther and Mordecai, Ruth and Naomi are some of the pairings which come to mind. A good example comes in the *Acts of the Apostles* when St. Paul heals the crippled man from Lystra.

> *And when the people saw what Paul had done, they lifted up their voices, saying in the speech of Lycaonia, 'the gods are come down to us in the likeness of men.' And they called Barnabas, Jupiter; and*

20

Paul, Mercurius, because he was the chief speaker.
Acts 14:2

Kabbalah places the planet Jupiter on the sefira of *Hesed* on the right-hand pillar of the Tree of Life and Mercury on the sefira of *Hod* on the left-hand pillar.

When Jesus speaks what is probably his most famous 'I Am' statement, "I am the way, the truth and the life" (John 14:6), he names the Greek translations of three of the Hebrew names of the sefirot: *the Way* being Hod on the left-hand pillar, *the Life* being *Nezah* on the right-hand pillar, and the Truth being *Tiferet* in the heart of the Tree of Life. Tiferet is the reflection of Yahweh Elohim, the Holy One, the Creator, and all the sefirot below are unique offspring of the Divine Mother and the Sacred Father. In the New Testament the Virgin Mary, impregnated by the Holy Spirit and giving birth to the Divine child, tells this story in a simplified form in a way that both enchants the listener with its magical promise of hope and informs the mystic that the writers understood the use of the great Cosmic pattern behind the design and teachings of the First Temple.

The Gospels of the New Testament would appear to be kabbalistic in design and content as well as a reflection of the teaching and structure of the Hebrew First Temple. There are four Canonical Gospels – Matthew, Mark, Luke and John – reflecting the four winds, the four zones of the world,[7] the four courts of the Temple and, to the Kabbalist, the Four Worlds of Jacob's Ladder.

Chapter Three

Literal Truths

The teachings of the Bible are a mixture of history, myth and legend. The very same stories, under different guises, appear in the myths of all the religions of the world; they all feature archetypal people facing similar situations. Some of these stories are based on recorded facts; others cannot be traced throughout the chronicles of history.

Centuries of selected focus on parts of the Bible have not helped our perceptions. It is an incomplete study just to use the bits that we can handle and ignore the others. I remember a friend who was a church-going Christian saying quite happily that she ignored a lot of the Gospels because she didn't like the content.

The great – and little – truths in spiritual teachings are revealed in what is not expressly stated. It is up to us to look at the spaces between the words and the intention behind them and, to do that, we need to overcome many prejudices that have been formed by reading the words alone. We also have to read this ancient book through the social and economic filters of its time.

The Bible was written more than 2000 years ago. Whether or not we believe that it is the unadulterated word of God, the fact that we are looking at an ancient text through modern eyes means that we cannot see it as it was originally written or as we were intended to understand it.

We have very little knowledge of the mind-set or the lifestyles of those who wrote it or of those who heard it. It's important to appreciate that very few people read it for themselves; the Torah in particular was read out loud, not only because so few people could read but also so that it would not be over-analyzed through repeated reading of the same lines. We need to attempt at least to assess each teaching according to the social laws of the times. If we choose to read at four different levels, that should be easier than it seems. While cultural patterns may change, Universal Law does not.

Some people wonder whether God evolves with humanity; others are certain that God is Absolute and perfect and cannot evolve. What is certain is that humanity's ability to understand God, the world and the Universe *has* evolved – even to the extent of many of us being able to live freely in a society that no longer requires us to believe in any God at all and does not punish us for that disbelief. By the law of cause and effect, as our perception of God evolves, so will our experience of God.

The Bible stories are our story. If they repulse us, it is because some truth within them hurts us or because we do not understand them. We have all the aspects of what we see to be a judgmental God within ourselves, and that perception can draw negative experiences to ourselves because of our beliefs, thoughts and actions.

As to what is relevant in the Bible to the stories of the women we are to examine, the best place to start is with a quotation from Proverbs, the inspiration for the title of this book. This version is from the Hebrew prayer book given to me by my Jewish mother-in-law, Miriam Clark, and it is a beautiful Hebrew Testament view of a woman's worth:

A woman of worth, who can find? For her price is far above rubies. The heart of her husband trusts in her and he shall have no lack of gain. She does him good and not evil all the days of her life. She seeks wool and flax and works willingly with her hands. She is like the merchant ships; she brings her food from afar. She rises also while it is yet night and sets forth provision for her household and their portion for her maidens. She considers a field and buys it: with the fruit of her hands she plants a vineyard. She girds her loins with strength and makes strong her arms. She perceives that her earnings

are good: her lamp goes not out by night. She puts her hands to the
distaff and her hands hold the spindle. She puts out her hand to the
poor: yea, she puts forth her hands to the needy. She is not afraid of
the snow for her household for all her household are clothed with
scarlet. She makes for herself coverings of tapestry; her clothing is
fine linen and purple. Her husband is known in the gates when he
sits among the elders of the land. She makes linen garments and sells
them; and delivers girdles unto the merchant. Strength and majesty
are her clothing and she laughs at the time to come. She opens her
mouth with wisdom and the law of loving-kindness is on her tongue.
She looks well to the ways of her household and eats not the bread of
idleness. Her children rise up and call her blessed; her husband also
and he praises her, saying: 'Many daughters have done worthily but
you excel them all.' Favour is false and beauty is vain but a woman
that fears the Lord, she shall be praised. Give her of the fruit of her
hands and let her works praise her in the gates.
Proverbs 31:10-31[8]

Worthy women were seen as kind, sensible, prosperous, indus-
trious, innovative, loved and appreciated. But they were also
seen as rare.

The Life and Times of Women in Biblical Days

In Biblical times, the most important thing for a wife to do was
produce children to secure the tribal line. As a general rule, girls
were married at around 14 years old and probably died before 40.
The average lifespan for a woman in cosmopolitan Rome at the
time of Jesus was 27 years[9] so it is likely to have been similar in
the Jewish Kingdoms. Romantic love would have been rare; there
would have been very little opportunity to sigh and wish and
hope for the ideal mate. You were a success – according to social,
family and tribal law – if you produced children and survived
childbirth.

However, despite the commentaries' laudatory words for the

Matriarchs, there are plenty of negatives in the observations of the scribes. The Midrash says, in its interpretation of the story of Abraham and Sarah, that women have four main traits. They are greedy, eavesdroppers, slothful and envious.[10]

To add to that there are three more intrinsically feminine traits: being talkative, being scratchers, being prone to steal and prone to 'gadding about'.

The 'evidence' of these eight sins in the commentary are:

- Eve was greedy. *"She took of the fruit thereof and did eat"* (Genesis 3:6).
- Sarah was an eavesdropper. *"And Sarah heard in the tent door"* (Genesis 18:10).
- Sarah was slothful. Abraham says to her *"make ready quickly three measures of fine meal"* (Genesis 18:6).
- Sarah was a scratcher. *"My scratch be upon thee"* (Genesis 16:5). This is a particularly challenging one as it comes from a Rabbinical interpretation of the Hebrew word *hamac* – wrong – being derived from *himmes*, to scratch. A more successful translation might be *"my wrong be upon thee."*
- Rachel was envious. *"Rachel envied her sister"* (Genesis 30:1).
  And prone to steal. *"And Rachel stole the idols"* (Genesis 31:19).
- Dinah (Leah's daughter) was a gadabout. *"And Dinah... went out to see the daughters of the land."* (Genesis 34:1)
- Miriam was talkative. *"And Miriam spoke against Moses"* (Numbers 12:1).

The commentaries certainly make much of the virtues of the women, mainly as good wives or mothers; they seek meaning in the texts in ways that are sometimes heart-warming and sometimes perturbing to our modern eyes. They also gloss over, or excuse, some of the women's problems saying, for example, that the barrenness that broke their hearts occurred *"so that their husbands might derive pleasure from them, for when a woman is with child she is disfigured and lacks grace."*[11] A parallel passage adds at this point that: *"as soon as Sarah conceived, her good looks faded."*[12]

They report on Karma – what goes around comes around – particularly in the case of Jacob who deceives his father, Isaac, so that he can receive the blessing due to his brother Esau. Jacob is in turn tricked by his future father-in-law, Laban, into marrying his elder daughter, Leah, rather than the beloved younger one, Rachel.

In cases such as these, Midrash often takes a huge leap of faith to ascribe merciful and virtuous reasons behind what, on the surface, are cruel or selfish acts. In the case of the women this must be a desire – whether consciously realized or not – to show the Divine Feminine working within the women. For example, Genesis says simply that Jacob discovered too late that he had married Leah, not Rachel. Nothing is said about whether Rachel knew of this or what she felt. But Midrash explains that there was a plan hatched by Jacob and Rachel as they both knew that Laban might attempt to make the substitution of Leah as the heavily-veiled bride in order to have his elder daughter married first. Rachel was to have a crossed-fingers signal to show Jacob to ensure him that she was the right one, the one he loved. But when the deception was taking place, she gave that signal to Leah out of love for her sister whom she knew would be publicly humiliated if the truth came out before the consummation of the marriage.[13]

This is all total surmise. The Bible never once mentions, nor even implies, that Rachel loves either Leah or Jacob. How we read between those lines depends entirely on what picture we want to present and whatever we, ourselves, believe. As it is important that the Matriarchs are seen to be virtuous women, beautiful reasons are given. But it is also possible that their stories are more basic: that what Kabbalah would refer to as the lower psyche of the feminine (as well as the masculine) is likely to deceive another to get what it wants and to fight like cat and dog forevermore. There is value in all the levels of interpretation but it is important to not simply paint the unskillful behavior pink and simply pass it off as a level of spiritual love when it may actually be ego, pride or fear – emotions to which we can all relate.

At the literal level, it's easy enough to say that women were oppressed and subservient in Biblical times but, with the Bible in particular, we can find evidence to prove almost anything we want. The majority of the records we have about women's lives stated what people thought *should* be the correct behavior for women rather than what might actually have been happening. As with the news today, it is the discord that is commented on rather than the harmony, and it is the calls for change that hit the headlines rather than the everyday contentment or working practice. It's rare that something is condemned or forbidden if it isn't already happening.

The Levels of Freedom for Women

It is fairly clear from the documentation we have that Jewish women had more freedom than either their Greek or Roman sisters. However, our modern filter of what is correct both politically and socially might still assume that they were oppressed, and we must always consider the fact that our information refers mostly to the middle and aristocratic classes. Greek women of the higher echelons rarely went out of the house except to religious ceremonies; Roman women did not go out alone (they were accompanied by slaves or male relatives). A Greek citizen's wife and higher-ranking Greek women were mostly confined to the home apart from religious duties when they would be accompanied by a male relative. They owned no property and were rarely educated – apart from the women of Sparta. Roman women of the higher classes could go out of the home if accompanied by a male relative or slave, and Roman daughters were taught basic counting skills, herbal lore and manners. Roman and Jewish women were at the heart of domestic life and, if their external power was limited, their power within the family was real including acting as 'regents' for sons who were under age if their mothers were widowed.[14]

The New Testament carries many references to strong and wealthy women and many of them were Jewesses. The greatest advantage these women had over both Roman and Greek women was that Jewesses could own land and property. If they married, this land belonged to their husbands, as was the case throughout most of the Western world until the 19th century, but on widowhood or divorce it returned to their ownership. The Gospel of Luke states that Jesus was supported by wealthy women.

And certain women, which had been healed of evil spirits and infirmities, Mary called Magdalene, out of whom went seven devils, and Joanna the wife of Chuza, Herod's steward, and Susanna, and many others, which ministered unto him of their substance.
Luke 8:2

The word for substance is *huparchonta* meaning 'possessions, goods, wealth, property'.

All the commentaries, histories and accounts of women that we read from Biblical times were written by men. Many of them were written by scribes or aesthetes or those of a priestly caste. We do not have the views of the women on women from historical times either but we can, surely, see them echoed in the modern world where women are sometimes harder on their sisters than anyone else.

The Jewish women in Biblical days may not have worshipped very much at Temple or studied sacred words or texts. Instead they worked at the cutting-edge of faith, at the times of birth, death and sickness. If they didn't understand herbal lore themselves, they knew someone who did. And it would be on their own priestesses – or Rebbitzen – that they would have called in times of crisis. The Rebbitzen was traditionally the Rabbi's wife. She was the one in charge at the *Mikvah*, the women's ritual baths. *Mikvaot* were used for ritual cleansing, especially after events and situations that rendered the Hebrews 'unclean'. Women outside of orthodox Jewry often feel a revulsion for the idea that a woman is expected to be cleansed after her menstruation before she can return to her husband's bed but the laws of purity also required any shedding of blood to be similarly ritually dissolved, as it also required any pus or seeping to be subjected to the same rules. In a desert society, such as that of the Hebrews' in the Wilderness during the Exodus from Egypt, the scent of blood attracted pests; infection and fly-blown wounds were often fatal; diseases spread like wildfire and great care was needed around the sick and the dying.

These ritual baths may have been a delight – we are so cosseted with our daily baths and showers that we cannot possibly realize the spiritual, psychological and physical value of a monthly immersion in fresh, running water.

Living water was always important to the Hebrew people both in the desert, where it was said to follow Miriam, and in the Temple where its sacred heart, the Holy of Holies, contained a stream of fresh, running water.

Home Ritual and Belief

Historical accounts of religious practice focus on services at temple, synagogue and church but little is written about the simple, everyday worship and ritual in the home. We do know of the Jewish Sabbath Eve service, the closing of the Sabbath and other home rituals but the most important spiritual rituals that would have concerned women in Biblical days were 'unclean' subjects in Jewish Law, and not publicly debated by men.

Time-honored rituals, handed down from mother to daughter and villager to villager, would have accompanied fertility, lactation, childcare, dealing with disease, menstruation, birth and death. None of these were written down because they were unlikely to have been revealed to the men. Indeed, many of the rituals might have been prevented by the priests and the rabbis had they known of them. An herb to stop a pregnancy in a woman already wounded by repeated childbirth would not have been tolerated openly in a society which believed that one of the greatest commandments was to *be fruitful and multiply"* (Genesis 1:22). Instead they would have been given secretly and with a compassion greater than Law.

Nowadays, of course, much of what the women did with herbs and salves is known as medicine and, with the advent of science, such drugs can be manufactured, the origins often unfortunately derided as 'alternative' medicine. We forget, for example, that our modern aspirin derives from the bark of the willow tree.

The women had knowledge of herbs and rituals – and they were not above invoking magic if the need arose. We know from the story of Rachel and Leah that mandrake root could boost fertility (Genesis 30:14). They also used henbane and hollyhock for pain as well as poppy syrup, a forerunner of morphine or heroin. Carob was useful for diarrhea; elecampane root could bring up phlegm and help with relaxation and sleep; hyssop salved coughs and hyssop flowers mixed with goldenrod formed a useful damp poultice for burns. Ergot, a fungus that grows on rye, could start or increase labor; mistletoe, tansy and chrysanthemum had powerful and extremely dangerous abortive powers, to be used only when the mother's life was in danger; and strangleweed was used as a contraceptive, dried, crushed and boiled in water.[15]

"Forsake not the law of thy mother" says Proverbs 6:20; and in

Ezekiel 16:14 the Lord reminds Israel of the importance of cutting the baby's umbilical cord and washing, salting and swaddling the child – all the work of the women, as was circumcision: *"Then Zipporah took a sharp stone, and cut off the foreskin of her son"* (Exodus 4:25).

The Hebrew Testament is about the followers of one God with many aspects and in both the Hebrew Testament and in archaeology there is evidence that the women in particular did call on 'lesser gods'.

In Genesis, Rachel steals her father's *teraphim*, or idols, and in the *First Book of Samuel*, Michal, wife of David, places a household *teraph*, together with a bolster, in David's bed to deceive her father, King Saul, who intends to kill him (1 Samuel 19:13).

Archaeologists have discovered thousands of figurines of women, dating back to the times of the monarchs of Israel, within the houses in villages and towns across Israel and Palestine. The majority of these clay and terracotta images are naked from the waist up, holding their breasts with their hands. Below the waist there is nothing but a pillar so they are unlikely to be fertility images. Those are thought to be represented by other statuettes depicting a couple in bed with each other, which have also been found – but these are far fewer in number.

Scholars disagree on their representation as goddesses because they do not wear crowns or ornaments.[16] It is generally thought that they represent the women on Earth; the ones who are asking and invoking for help – and that the images continue the prayers of the women who have asked for help or guidance. However, as we shall see in the next chapter, the Divine Feminine in the form of Asherah or the Elohim was depicted in the First Temple as a pillar so it is quite possible that these images are of her.

One male figure that the women are believed to have used has also been found in quantity within the archaeology of the time of the Kingdoms – *Bes*, an Egyptian god, who was believed to protect women in childbirth together with newborn babies.

Life in Biblical times was often nasty, brutish and short, but the knowledge of a Divine Mother or feminine source of inspiration would have been of much help in the matters which were outside the realm of the 'clean' and the masculine.

Chapter Four

The Divine Feminine

The great American mystic Joseph Campbell wrote of four historical stages of belief in the principles of creation. These are:

1. A world born of a goddess without consort.
2. A world born of a goddess made fertile by a consort.
3. A world fashioned from the body of a goddess by a male warrior-god alone.
4. A world created by the unaided power of a male god alone.[17]

Although it may appear to be almost wholly patriarchal when it comes to God, in the Hebrew language the Bible is not as partisan as it appears. The Elohim, who creates the Universe according to the first two chapters of Genesis, is a feminine Hebrew noun with a plural masculine ending. This implies the second stage of belief – that the Divine Feminine was made fertile by the Divine Masculine.

Certainly the One God which has come down to us through conventional Judaism, Christianity and Islam is not the whole story. Kabbalah teaches that there are ten aspects of God, one for each of the sefirot. Some traditions speak of the 72 names of God, derived from a sequence of 72 specially-arranged letters found in the Biblical *Book of Exodus* (14:19–21). This sequence is also made up from three verses of 72 letters each. To be strictly accurate it is a 72-*syllable* name of God which is part of a 216-letter name of God.

What is becoming clear through the work of modern-day scholars of the Bible is that, in the time of the First Temple, the Lord had a wife. Her name was *Ashratah* (Hebrew form) or

Asherah (the more commonly-used Ugaritic form). She was also known as the Holy One, the Queen Mother, the Living Almighty, the Queen of Heaven, Sophia or Wisdom. She had her own worshippers in the first Jewish Temple.

This Divine Partner was exiled during the purge of the Temple in the seventh century BCE but a god cannot be banished from the hearts and minds of people. Although the sacred feminine may have been exiled, she refused to go. She is mourned in the *Book of Jeremiah* (44:18): *"But since we left off to burn incense to the queen of heaven, and to pour out drink offerings unto her, we have wanted all things, and have been consumed by the sword and by the famine."* And she returns in the *Book of Revelation* (12:1):*"And there appeared a great wonder in heaven; a woman clothed with the sun, and the moon under her feet, and upon her head a crown of twelve stars."*

Her stories have also blended in with the pantheons of Greek, Roman, Hindu and Norse gods, the esoteric tradition and, to a certain extent, in the Catholic Church. In the 21st century she came back with a bang in such diverse ways as *The Da Vinci Code* or the Goddess Temple in the British town of Glastonbury.

But let's take a step back before we consider the exiling of the Goddess. First, we need to note that she was the wife of *The Lord* and not the wife of *God*, God in this particular aspect meaning the Source, the All.

The Source of All has no gender. It is Unity. It is beyond existence; it fills all things. It can never be portrayed as masculine or feminine; it is incomprehensible; ineffable. But the fact that Biblical Hebrew, the original language of the texts that have influenced Judaism, Christianity and Islam for centuries, has no neuter grammatical gender meant that God was referred to by the scribes as 'He'.

On the Tree of Life (fig. 1, fig. 3) *Keter*, the crown of the sefirot, represents the One Source of All. From Keter springs Hokhmah, the place of Wisdom and Inspiration. This is named for Yahweh, the aspect of God known as the Lord (spelt with capital letters in the Hebrew Testament). From Hokhmah springs Binah, the place of Understanding, named for the Elohim. Binah is the holding force for the explosive aspect of Hokhmah. Without her, the wisdom could not be transmitted. What Hokhmah reveals, Binah translates. She is the face of wisdom; the Great Mother who can explain and interpret the word of the Lord.

From these three sefirot, which make up what is known as the Supernal Triad, flows the whole of creation. Binah, as the Elohim, is both singular and plural: "Goddess receiving God and giving birth to gods."

The name 'Elohim' is repeated thirty-two times in the creation story of Genesis, giving the form to the Tree of Life which has ten sefirot linked by twenty-two paths. The purpose of these is to pour the light of Divinity through the whole of creation. As each sefira/vessel is filled with divine light, it overflows and pours the light on. "My cup runneth over," sings the psalmist in Psalm 23.

Yahweh turns up only in Genesis Chapter Two – firstly as Yahweh Elohim. Only in Chapter Four does He turn up on his own for the purposes of human procreation:

And Adam knew Eve his wife; and she conceived, and bare Cain, and said, 'I have gotten a man from the Lord [Yahweh].'
Genesis 4:1

From then on, we have a mixture of names for God/the Lord/the Lord God but we are only properly introduced in the *Book of Exodus* at the Burning Bush.

The Queen of Heaven

From this synthesis of 'one God, many aspects' came a First Temple theology of acknowledging the male and female aspects of the Divine. Yahweh, the masculine right-hand pillar in the Temple, received offerings of wine, and Elohim, Ashratah or Asherah, the feminine left-hand pillar, received offerings of bread. For the sake of convenience, we will call her 'Asherah' from now on.

The fact that Asherah and her brother/husband/partner existed tells us that even in a great monotheistic faith we have a fundamental need to express both the masculine and feminine aspects of ourselves. Just because you are a woman doesn't mean you don't have masculine aspects, and just because you are a man doesn't mean you don't embrace the feminine.

We truly have very little idea what the worship or, more likely, reverence to Asherah consisted of but legend tells us that women would weave colored scarves and banners to place on or around her pillar in the temple and the Bible appears to confirm that: *"the women wove hangings for the grove [asherah]"* Kings 23:7.

One of the reasons that she has been derided for centuries and downgraded is because a goddess of the same or similar name appears in so many different faiths. There are certainly many religious and historical confusions around Asherah. The best-known archaeological evidence for her existence as the consort of the Lord comes from the excavations at Kuntillet Ajrud, in the northern Sinai desert, where a storage jar shows three anthropomorphic figures and an inscription that refers to "Yahweh... and [his] Asherah."

The name Asherah appears to originate from the city of Akkad, one of the ancient sites of Mesopotamia. It has other forms, such as Asherdu(s) or Ashertu(s) or Aserdu(s) or Asertu(s) in Hittite. Asherah is generally considered identical with the Ugaritic goddess Athirat (more accurately transcribed as 'Aṯirat). Both are mother goddesses. Ugarit was a city in Syria; in modern days it is known as Ras Shamra.

In the Ugaritic texts (before 1200 BCE) Athirat is almost always given her full title *rbt 'aṯrt ym, rabat 'Aṯirat yammi,* 'Lady Athirat of the Sea' or, as more fully translated, 'She who treads on the sea.'

Her other main divine epithet was *'qaniyatu 'ilhm',* which may be translated as 'the creatrix of the gods' which is similar to the concept of the Elohim.

In Ugaritic documents dating back to 1200 BCE, Athirat is clearly distinguished from Ashtart/Astarte/Ashtoreth, Asherah and Anath. In non-Ugaritic sources from later periods the distinction between the goddesses and their names becomes blurred.

A first link with Christianity can be seen in that the name of the Virgin Mary, who is also known in Catholicism as the Queen of Heaven, would, in Hebrew, have been Mara-yam (Miriam). This meant 'strong sea' or 'bitter waters' according to the use of vowels in the original consonants. The latter is very similar to 'She who treads on the sea', especially as Mary gave birth to a son who could walk on water.

'The Queen of Heaven', however, is a title given to many Goddesses including the Egyptian Isis and the Sumerian goddess Inanna. These women were mothers of the King/Lord as well as wives of the King/Lord. Mary was with child by *Hagios Pneuma*, the Holy Spirit, according to the Gospel of Matthew. In Luke, the angel says instead, *"ho kurios meta sou"* – "the Lord is with thee." And that she has found *"charis para Theos"* – "the grace (or favor) of God."

Apart from one reference to Jesus as "my Lord and my God" by the disciple Thomas in John 20:28, Jesus is always referred to as 'Lord' in lower case letters. The kabbalistic interpretation of Thomas' use of the word 'God' would be that, as John is the Gospel of the Divine World of Azilut, its entire content is raised to the mystical level, whereas the Synoptic Gospels of Matthew (Asiyyah), Mark (Yezirah) and Luke (Beriah) are the literal, allegorical and metaphysical realms. In John we see Jesus as the icon – the window – through which God speaks as the *Logos* or the Word.

Both Jewish and Greek mystical and philosophical traditions understand God to be nothing that we can define; nothing that is, in fact, anything. So the names of God with which we are juggling are just that: *names* of God; not God Itself.[18]

So Mary is both wife and mother to the Lord. She may even be wife or mother to God but only of the *named aspects of God*, not the totality of the Unknowable One. This is not to deride her or Jesus. We humans need images and ideas to focus on in order to come close to comprehending the Divine. Each of the Gospels provides a different window for viewing Christ. Matthew provides lineage through Joseph, not Mary, and concentrates on physical healings and miracles. Mark speaks only of the development of Jesus as a Messianic being; he has no interest in the Nativity. The miracles of Mark are of the cleansing of demons – psychological entities. Luke is the spiritual Gospel – the Gospel of the women, seeing them having the same importance as the men. Luke steps out of the tribal world. There are nineteen stories of the women in Luke and this is the Gospel where the Divine Feminine comes into her own with the Virgin birth and the nativity that we celebrate at Christmas. Here, Jesus is no longer the suffering servant; he does not cry out in distress on the cross: "My God, my God, why hast thou forsaken me?" but instead says, "Father, forgive them; they know not what they do."

The Exclusion of the Divine Feminine

Asherah was removed from the First Temple in the reign of King Josiah in 622 BCE. Thirty years before the Babylonian exile, the High Priest, Hilkiah, found a copy of the book of the law in the Temple (sources differ on whether it was the whole first five books of the Hebrew Testament or just the *Book of Deuteronomy*). The book was read to the King Josiah who rent his clothes with grief and said:

> Go ye, enquire of the Lord for me, and for the people, and for all
> Judah, concerning the words of this book that is found: for great is
> the wrath of the Lord that is kindled against us, because our fathers

have not hearkened unto the words of this book, to do according unto all that which is written concerning us.
2 Kings 22:13

His servants went to Huldah the prophetess who told them that the Lord God was angry at the burning of incense to other gods (*elohim*). Josiah then ordered a purge of the Temple, intending to remove all evidence of any god other than the Lord. That there must have been worship of other gods – or other aspects of the One God – in the Temple itself is implicit. He did not succeed fully, for the Queen of Heaven was clearly lamented in many places within the rest of the Hebrew Testament.

She wasn't the only one who went:

And the high places that were before Jerusalem, which were on the right hand of the mount of corruption, which Solomon the king of Israel had builded for Ashtoreth the abomination of the Zidonians, and for Chemosh the abomination of the Moabites, and for Milcom the abomination of the children of Ammon, did the king defile. And he brake in pieces the images, and cut down the groves [asherah].
2 Kings 23:13

A new temple was in the process of being built at the time of the Babylonian invasion and once the Hebrews returned to their land in 538 BCE, the new king, Ezra, built a very much plainer temple possibly, partly, because of financial constraints. The purge itself was a similar event to the British Reformation where the Catholic Church was overthrown, followed by the Puritan ethic of the Cromwellian winners of the Civil War. In England, Catholicism was replaced by Protestantism and, later, Puritanism where the Roundheads destroyed images of saints and the Virgin in churches throughout the British Isles.

There's little doubt that there was much corruption within Catholicism in the days of the British Reformation, not least the selling of 'indulgences' which was forgiveness at a price. Although the reaction was extreme there was a reason behind it. So it is fair to surmise that the first Temple of the Hebrews may also have become corrupt and the Elohim may have morphed into a series of cults. Josiah certainly banned the practice of child sacrifice (2 Kings 23:10). This had happened over the centuries but it is not exactly clear whether it was done at, or through, the Temple or only in the worship of other gods.

What we do know is that when the energy of the Goddess was banished from the first Temple, the teachings about many things concerning what is now seen to be the orthodox Jewish faith changed. The story of Moses and the Exodus became a prime focus and the feminine was transformed from being powerful and essential to dark, controlling and bad. Other aspects of the early worship such as divination, soothsaying, wizardry and sorcery were also banned – and became associated with the feminine.

The Asherah may have been gone; but she was not forgotten. Her name reappears in many places throughout the Hebrew Testament – sometimes as an almond tree, frequently as a grove of sacred trees or poles near an altar (a grove in Hebrew is an *asherah*). In the *Book of Deuteronomy* there is an injunction that all places of worship on mountains and hills and under living trees should be destroyed. This 'pagan' worship was either associated with or confused with the Tree of Life. Mishnah makes it clear that during the Feast of Tabernacles which features bowers made of branches, no branch from an asherah may be used.[19] An asherah is elsewhere defined as a tree that had been planted or specially shaped for the purposes of worship.[20]

Shekhinah

Despite the exile of the Queen of Heaven, there are still two aspects of the sacred feminine within Judaism that have long been deeply respected. They are Wisdom and Shekhinah.

It is very likely that all Hebrew women in Biblical days knew about Shekhinah whether that was the name given to her or not; it was Shekhinah who gave birth to souls into the world and received them back into the heavens at death. Shekhinah is a Hebrew word variously translated as 'radiance' and 'dwelling place'. Kabbalists and other mystics refer to it as 'the presence of God'. It is said to reside both in the heart of God and in the soul of a woman. On the Tree of Life, it is placed on the Malkhut (Kingdom) of Azilut (God) as the feminine aspect of Adonai, the Lord (this aspect is spelt in lower case in the Hebrew Testament whereas Yahweh is spelt in upper case as the LORD).

By the time the Talmud, the commentary on the Torah, was crystallized in writing in the second century CE, it was acknowledged that a man could not be regarded as complete without a wife for Shekhinah could only live in him through his relationship with her. This is explained in the *Zohar* or *Book of Splendor*, a companion Talmud with deeper mystical teachings. Its origin is disputed: the *Zohar* was only revealed to the public in the thirteenth century and debate continues as to whether it was written then by the man who discovered it in Spain, Moses de Leon, or if the book is a genuine tract from the second century written by Rabbi Simeon ben Yochai. As it was written in the Aramaic of Yochai's time, it may well be genuine. More contemporary mystics might argue that the whole book was channeled via Moses de Leon but very few orthodox Jewish mystics would accept that theory.

The *Zohar* also emphasizes the importance of marriage, stating that when a man is apart from his wife, God sends the spiritual Shekhinah with him to keep him safe. When he is home with her, Shekhinah is automatically there, because of his wife's presence.[21]

The importance of the presence of the feminine to light the Sabbath candles on a Friday night is also emphasized in the *Zohar* in the story of how Rebekah brought the light back into

Abraham and Isaac's tent after the death of Sarah:

> *When a man is at home the principal element of his home is his wife,*
> *for the Shekhinah does not leave the home as long as his wife is there.*
> *For we have learned from the verse 'Isaac brought her into the tent*
> *of Sarah, his mother,' (Gen 24:67) that the lamp was kindled...*
> *Why? Because the Shekhinah came into the home.*[22]

To the Kabbalist, the Sabbath Eve ceremony represents the Four
Worlds of Jacob's Ladder and of Creation itself. These are the four
primary elements that the ancients were able to observe: the Fire
of the Sun; the Air of the sky; the Water of the clouds, seas and
rivers; and the Earth of the ground beneath them. Some ancient
civilizations added an extra element: Metal. This would represent
the meld of Earth and Fire for cultures that knew of fire within
the ground, such as volcanoes.

Each of these elements mingled with the others: the light and
heat of the Sun flowed through the air which, in turn, mingled
with water in rain. The water melded in the earth as mud and
clay.

The temples of ancient Israel, with four courtyards, were
founded on these four elements. Divinity was seen to be residing
in the court of Fire. Earth was the lowest and coarsest of the levels
with Fire as the highest and finest.

At the Sabbath Eve service, the woman lighting the candles
becomes Shekhinah, the feminine aspect of the Divine which
links heaven and earth. By lighting the light and drawing the
presence down to her home, she performs *Kabbalat Shabbat,*
bringing in 'the Sabbath Bride' – Divinity – to transform the
mundane into the holy. This essence lasts throughout the
Sabbath. Once she has spoken the sacred prayers of blessing, she
then pours wine (representing the second World of Air because of
its fermentation and scent) for her husband, imbuing the next
level with the Light of the Divine. He takes the ceremony down

through the lower World of Water, through the washing of hands and then to the lowest World, the Earth, represented by the salting and blessing of the bread. In orthodox Judaism, the husband will continue the blessing at the synagogue after the Sabbath eve meal.

This is very similar to the Roman ceremonies involving Vesta the goddess of the hearth (the sacred flame) and Janus, her partner, the god of the doorway. Vesta was responsible for the home and Janus for dealing with the outside world. Vesta had no distinct personality, played no part in the Roman myths and was never depicted in an image or a statue; but she was immensely powerful, not least through her priestesses, the Vestal Virgins, who were the only women in the Roman Empire who were assigned Senatorial status. If a convicted felon should encounter a Vestal Virgin on his way to jail or execution, and touch her, this was seen as a sign of Grace and his sin would be forgiven. However, a Vestal Virgin who lost her virginity suffered a terrible fate. No one was permitted to kill a Vestal Virgin but she would be buried alive in a chamber with food and left to suffocate.

The word Shekhinah does not appear in the Bible but it is woven among the commentaries and the mystical kabbalistic texts, and the essence of Shekhinah runs throughout Jewish tradition. The feminine, being hidden, secret and powerful and concerned with birth and death was sacred and, therefore, quite possibly intimidating or frightening to the everyday mind.

This may be a primal truth of why the feminine within any religious tradition may be feared: it is the inner, sacred teaching, not the outer form. It has to be sought-after; it is not to be revealed to just anyone but only to the genuine spiritual seeker. So those who complain that the feminine within a religion is nonexistent or hidden away could be missing the whole point. It was never meant to be handed to you on a plate; it is far too valuable for that.

According to Rabbinic tradition, the Shekhinah shares in the exile of the Jewish people. Or, perhaps more accurately, in the exile of all those who are apart from the original Temple. That would be interpreted as any spiritual seeker who searches for his or her own truth in a world where the sacred is perhaps less respected than it ever has been.

Wisdom

Wisdom is an acknowledged aspect of the Divine Feminine within the Hebrew Testament.

She is a tree of life to them that lay hold upon her: and happy is every one that retaineth her. The Lord by wisdom hath founded the earth; by understanding hath he established the heavens.
Proverbs 3:18–19

Wisdom is also a goddess. In Greek she is Sophia and in Hebrew, Hokhmah (sometimes spelt with a 'ch' instead of 'h' for the guttural sound). Both are feminine nouns. Wisdom pervades the Hebrew Testament and, in kabbalistic terms, she is the first vessel to receive the light of creation as it flowed (masculine-active) from the One. Hokhmah received it (feminine), filled her vessel and then flowed it on (masculine) to Binah, or Understanding. From there, all the lower sefirot were filled in turn in a dance between feminine and masculine. The relationship between Hokhmah and Binah is also referred to in Proverbs:

Get wisdom, get understanding: forget it not; neither decline from the words of my mouth. Forsake her not, and she shall preserve thee: love her, and she shall keep thee. Wisdom is the principal thing; get wisdom: and with all thy getting get understanding.
Proverbs 4:5–7

Without one, you cannot have the other.

Wisdom is also referred to in the *Book of Enoch*, a testament dating back to approximately 300 BCE and widely known at the time of the selection of the books for the Hebrew Canon. It was rejected within Judaism and, although it forms part of the canon of the Ethiopian and Eritrean Orthodox Churches and was referred to by many of the first Christian Church Fathers, it was also rejected by Christianity in the fourth century CE when St. Jerome compiled the Vulgate Bible. However, it is quoted in the New Testament *Book of Jude*.

In *Enoch*, the prophet is shown the wonders of the Universe by the four archangels associated with the Temple and with Jacob's Ladder: Michael, Raphael, Gabriel and Uriel.

At one point, at the heart of these miraculous visions, he sees a Messianic figure and says,

And in that place I saw the fountain of righteousness which was inexhaustible: And around it were many fountains of wisdom: And all the thirsty drank of them, and were filled with wisdom.
Chapter 48:1

Moving natural water sources were very important to the Hebrews – their sacred cleansing rituals were always performed in running water. Still water could cleanse the body but only flowing water, imbued with air, could cleanse psyche and spirit.

Enoch also sees two trees which are glorious and fragrant. The first is the Tree of Life, shown to him by Michael who says that no human may touch it until the end of days. The second is the Tree of Knowledge.

I said: 'How beautiful is the tree, and how attractive is its look!' Then Raphael the holy angel, who was with me, answered me and said: 'This is the tree of wisdom, of which thy father old (in years) and thy aged mother, who were before thee, have eaten, and they learnt wisdom and their eyes were opened, and they knew that they

were naked and they were driven out of the garden.'
1 Enoch 32:6

Michael represents the Divine World of Azilut, to where we aspire to return, the home of Adam Kadmon, the place of perfected humanity; Raphael represents Beriah, the World of spirit and the highest level that ordinary humans can attain.

So here we have an apparent contradiction as to whether Wisdom is the Tree of Life or the Tree of Knowledge. The accepted Biblical texts say that it is the former but oral memories are long and, if Wisdom is deeply associated with the feminine and this has also been linked with the Tree of Knowledge, the source of the first disobedience, we may have here another ancient reason for the distrust of the feminine. However, it is also worth considering that if we do have the knowledge of good and evil, then we are in profound need of the wisdom to discern the difference between our own opinions and the rules of society about what is good or bad, and the deep spiritual truths.

Certainly, with the ending of the First Temple, the Divine Feminine fell from Grace and her sacred worship became an abomination. Even Wisdom was seen as corrupted; the Tree of Life interpreted as the Tree of Knowledge. This is personified in the advent of a character whose effect has been far-reaching but who, like the *Book of Enoch*, was never even a part of the Bible. Her name is Lilith.

Part Two

Before the Descent

Chapter Five

Missing the Mark – Lilith

Name: Lilith is what is known as a *hapax legomenon*, which means a word that occurs only once in the Hebrew Bible and therefore cannot be defined by reference to the other times it is used. Generally it is said to mean 'of the night' which is quite a stretch as it is taken from the Hebrew word *laylah*, meaning 'night'. Other scholars prefer to use the Assyrian 'lilitu' meaning a female demon.

Lilith is the arch-demoness in the story of creation. She is not named in Genesis but legend still says she was Adam's first wife and the first archetype of the feminine mentioned in the Bible.

Lilith may appear only by inference but the echo of her presence has resounded down the centuries.

The Lilith legend is not originally Hebraic. Like Asherah, it would appear to have been made up from an amalgamation of ancient Babylonian and Assyrian beliefs that pervaded Mesopotamia. In Babylonian and Assyrian mythology, the male *lilu* and the female *lilitu* were demons that haunted deserts and were considered to be a threat to pregnant women and their babies. The similar *ardat-lili* was a demonic female who made men impotent and women sterile.

The story of Lilith was most likely to have been adopted by the Hebrews during the Babylonian captivity which followed after the end of the First Temple and the expulsion of the Divine Feminine. Some believed the exile came because they had purged the Temple, and others that it was because of the evils perpetrated from before the elimination of the old order.

The only reference to Lilith by name in the Bible is in Isaiah 34:14. Although the prophet lived in the 8th century BCE and the early part of the book is believed to date back to the 7th century, at least two thirds of the *Book of Isaiah* was written during and after the end of the Babylonian captivity[23] so it is worth speculating whether the adaptation of Babylonian and Syrian myths to form a Hebrew legend was a part of the demonizing of the old Temple order.

It is a description of desolation, nettles and brambles and dragons:

The wild beasts of the desert shall also meet with the wild beasts of the island, and the satyr shall cry to his fellow; the screech owl also shall rest there, and find for herself a place of rest.
Isaiah 34:13

The word translated as 'screech owl' is *liyliyth*. The King James Bible, following the Vulgate, defines 'the lilith' as 'the night demon', translating it from *lili* – the Hebrew word for night.

Hebrew etymology derives 'Lilith' from *layil*, 'night', but both Hebrew and Arabian folklore refer to her as a hairy night-monster. This even led to an Arabic story that Solomon suspected the Queen of Sheba of being Lilith because she had hairy legs! The original Lilith was said to be beautiful down to the waist and a monster below, which is quite probably a legend rooted in the fear of feminine sexuality.

Arabic legends show *Alilat* or *al-Lat* (a form of Lilith) as a pre-Islamic Arabian goddess who is mentioned in the Qur'an (Sura 53:19). Before the time of the prophet Mohammad she was considered to be one of the daughters of Allah and equated with the goddesses Athena and Aphrodite. As with Athena, her symbol is an owl, representing wisdom.

Lilith is said to have been Adam's first wife.

So God created man in his image, in the image of God created he him; male and female created he them. And God blessed them, and God said unto them, 'be fruitful, and multiply, and replenish

the earth.'
Genesis 1:27

Most people of faith assume that humanity is already present on the physical earth at this stage in the process of creation but Kabbalah teaches that this is not so. Creation is still in progress and this part of the great plan is still taking place in the heavenly World. In Kabbalah this is the World of Beriah and it is the origin of concepts and ideas rather than actual physical manifestations. So the mystic would see this as the creation of the first concept of humanity containing both male and female within it as God Itself does. It's similar to the situation where we might have an idea to write a book; we've got the inspiration and the subject matter, and they are very powerful and compelling. However, we are not exactly quite sure how it's going to work out, how many chapters there will be or how the story will find its way from the start to the denouement. That comes later.

From this creation-idea the next stage would be the *formation* of the two separate humans as souls with separate identities, coloring, height, weight and mannerisms. This takes place in the World of Yezirah and is the fleshing out of the idea or concept; in the case of the book, the outlining of all the chapters, description of the characters and the location where it takes place. Once these are in place, there is no going back as the plot takes on a kind of life force of its own. In the case of humans, only once their form was finalized would come the making of the physical bodies that they would inhabit on Earth; in the case of the book, it would only become real when it was capable of being be read by another.

Regarding Genesis at these different levels makes more sense of its repetition of the story of creation. After the Beriatic creation comes the Yeziratic formation. *"And the Lord God formed man of the dust of the ground, and breathed into his nostrils the breath of life; and man became a living soul"* (Genesis 2:7). Another possible source for the name Lilith is *Lil*, a Sumerian word which meant 'breath', or 'spirit', and was borrowed by the Babylonians for the same use, becoming *lillitu*. One of their chief deities, *En-Lil*, is Lord of the *Lilim*, a host of ghostly spirits flying around. So, we should consider the idea that Lilith is the breath of God into Adam.

The word 'man' quoted above is the Hebrew '*adamah*' which means 'human'. It did not, in ancient days, automatically imply gender. This created being is still androgynous but it is now capable of becoming more than a concept.

"*And the Lord God said, it is not good that the man [human] should be alone; I will make him an help meet for him*" (Genesis 2:18). The story continues that Eve was formed from a rib of the original Adamah. And here the androgynous being becomes two separate genders.

But most readers take "*male and female he created them*" literally, believing that it was two separate beings. This first created, Beriatic but unformed feminine was an androgynous half of Adamah. But legend made her separate and feminine and she became Lilith, created as Adam's equal from the cosmic dust.

Most of the legends about the discord between Adam and Lilith say it began when Adam commanded Lilith to bow to him and she refused. Spanish Sephardic Jewish versions of the story say she wanted Adam's power as well as her own and that she refused to lie beneath Adam during sex. Whatever the origins of this legend, the common thread is that Lilith saw the instruction to bow to be one implying that she was lesser than her husband.

Lilith spoke the true, unspeakable name of God, left Adam and flew away to the kingdom of the demons. Adam complained to God, and the angels Senoi, Sansenoi and Sannangelof were sent to bring her back. She refused.

Both Lilith's anger and her punishment are said to take many horrific forms, which we don't need to go into in any depth here. She is said to have married the king of the demons and to have sworn to destroy the children of her rival Eve. To this day, in orthodox Jewish homes, tokens of Senoi, Sansenoi and Sannangelof are placed in the rooms of newborn children to protect them from Lilith's vengeance. Amulets are also hung which say *'Lilith abi'* – 'Lilith begone' which have been associated, much later, with the English word 'lullaby'.

This legendary Lilith was never born so she cannot die; she never descended from Beriah nor ate from the Tree of Knowledge so she never put on the 'coat of skin' of the physical World as Adam and Eve did.

Several hundred years after Isaiah, we find Talmudic writings that describe Lilith (now as a named demon, rather than a broad category) as an irresistibly seductive she-demon with wings and long hair which, when worn loose, was seen as a sign of wantonness. She seduces unwary men, then savagely kills the children she bears from them.

Midrash, the compilation of stories that fill in the gaps in the text of Torah and Talmud, says that Adam was so angry with Eve after they left the garden that he left her for several years, during which time he was seduced by demons (these were called 'lilith' as the name was still a generic category of demon). One tale says that a specific lilith called Penzai seduced Adam and became pregnant. Others warn that Lilith creates wet dreams.

The Alphabet of Ben Sira (circa 700 CE) melds together several of the legends, creating Lilith the child-slaying night-demon who seduces Adam. The *Zohar* claims that she became the wife of Samael, the Angel of Death or, alternatively, the wife of Satan.

Traditional versions of the legend have been used to demonstrate that any woman who refuses to take orders from a man, or second place in the world, is demonic. Understandably this has caused some fairly strong reaction and, at the opposite end of the scale, Lilith's legend has also been used by feminists to raise the banner of female power. However, no matter how well-intended it may have been, the feminist angle is just as tainted with the scent of bitterness and anger as the original legend and neither is of any help to us in sorting the problem of the feisty feminine. Fortunately, there are other ways to look at the story.

This refusal to bow and the wanting of Adam's power as well as her own are the negative aspects of the feminine which are still feared in powerful women today. But is this about power or control? There is a subtle difference. Why would anyone understanding their own power and divinity want to take away the authority of another?

The legend varies so frequently that it is hard to pin it down and there are no attempts to harmonize each version. The *Zohar* (19:a) says:

> At the same time Yahweh created Adam, he created a woman, Lilith, who like Adam was taken from the earth. She was given to Adam as his wife. But there was a dispute between them about a matter that when it came before the judges had to be discussed behind closed doors. She spoke the unspeakable name of Jehovah and vanished.

A less frequently-quoted part of the same book talks of Lilith being a spirit:

> There is a female, a spirit of all spirits, and her name is Lilith, and she was at first with Adam. And in the hour when Adam was created and his body became completed, a thousand spirits from the left side clung to that body until the Holy One, blessed be He, shouted at them and drove them away... And when Adam stood up, his female was attached to his side. And that holy spirit which was in him spread out to this side and that side, and grew here and there, and thus became complete. Thereafter the Holy One, blessed be He, sawed Adam into two, and made the female [Eve]. And He brought her to Adam in her perfection like a bride to the canopy. When Lilith saw this, she fled. And she is in the cities of the sea.
> Zohar 3:19

The Alphabet of Ben Sira is the source of all the stories that claims this dispute is about sex, and who went on top or not. The renowned Jewish Kabbalist, Gershom Scholem, believed that the author of the *Zohar* was Moses de Leon, not the 2nd century Rabbis credited with it, and that de Leon was aware of the *Alphabet's* version of Lilith and used it.[24]

Sex could only be the issue if this were a story taking place in the physical World and there is no strong evidence that this is the case; the story itself doesn't even exist in the Bible which does have a literal aspect. Far from it; there are two sources at least which refer to Lilith as 'spirit'. And the phrase 'behind closed doors' implies the hidden tradition. So how, at the other levels, can we examine this story?

Lilith and the Tree of Life

Conventional Kabbalah does not place Lilith directly onto the Tree of Life, rather equating her with one of the *Klippot* or *Qliphot* which are shells or husks that surround the sefirot and act as barriers or evil impulses that challenge us. Lilith's particular *Klippah* is placed at Malkhut, the lowest sefira of the Tree of Life – the furthest from the Divine source but the place where the Divine plan is made manifest. This relies on Lilith being a seductress – and the legends do imply that she seduces men in their sleep, leading to wet dreams – and it is true that the material world, with its attractions and physical pleasures, can distract us from our spiritual life. However, I would place her at Hokhmah which is the first sefira descending from the Source of Keter.

Hokhmah is traditionally known as Wisdom. However, it can also refer to the attributes of revelation, revolution, rebellion, jumping to conclusions and making flash decisions. Hokhmah is represented in astrology by Uranus, the Aquarian planet.

Each of the sefirot receives the Divine breath or light before flowing it on to the next. Therefore each sefira is both feminine (receptive) and masculine (active) in turn. "Male and female created he them both," would mean that Lilith was the first aspect to receive the light. She was the breath that filled the sefira. Evidence for this? She knew the unspoken name of God which Adam (one step further away) did not. Figuratively, she would have had to bend or bow to Adam in order to share her power. Why would she not do that?

Lurianic Kabbalah carries an answer to this in teaching that the sefirot, as they were originally emanated from God, were incomplete and weak so they shattered under the impact of the infinite light of creation. This shattering of the vessels, known as the *Shevirat ha-Kelim*, is said to be the reason why there is a lack of unity in the world and bad things happening to good people. The shattering rent apart the masculine and feminine aspects of creation, and is the cause of an external force of evil in the world (like the Christian devil) because the shards from the broken sefirot are negative energies.

Modern interpretations also teach that the vessels did not want to receive; they wanted to be like God and give – and that the world's healing will come through giving. This is undoubtedly true but we must be filled ourselves first, as giving from an empty vessel helps no one and exhausts the giver.

However, before Luria's theory, back in pre-16th century times, Kabbalists believed that when God made the Universe it was perfect: *"And God saw every thing that he had made, and, behold, it was very good"* (Genesis 1:31). No external devils or demons; just human free will and cause and effect.

So, perhaps the Lilith story is how the Babylonian exiles justified the terrible events that had happened to them. God had made a perfect world; they were good people and did not deserve their plight. Therefore there must be some external energy which was responsible. The Asherah would have been a soft target; the Temple had become corrupted and the feminine was seen as being to blame for that. Therefore it would have been a simple conclusion to draw that, in some way, the Divine Feminine was responsible for all their ills. In a female demoness who was strongly associated with heathen gods and who could be accused of attacking the innocent children of the righteous there was a scapegoat. Moreover, she would also stop women from becoming above themselves, thereby preventing any female calls for a return of their own Goddess. The idea of woman against woman could be the source of another of the legends about Lilith: that she was the original serpent in the Garden of Eden.[25]

Levels of Interpretation

It's a challenge to offer a literal interpretation of a story which is only apparent in the spaces between the words. But the drawing together of all the goddesses into a Lilith at the time of the Babylonian exile would have served a purpose. In all ages, humanity has needed someone or something to blame when things go wrong.

The allegorical or psychological story is the one that Lilith refused to bow to Adam. Here we can see that her behavior was similar to that of many of us in the modern world who feel demeaned if we are asked to give precedence to another. In that case, it was Lilith's lack of faith in her own power and her own Divinity which made her see Adam as superior and to interpret the command to bow to him as proof of her inferiority. This may be observed in the Western military forces where the junior officer salutes the senior officer first. But in the Eastern countries of the world, it is the great masters who bow first to their students. The host and hostess bow to the guests coming into their home. They are not bowing because they are inferior but because they are glad to welcome honored guests and they are allowing the Divinity within them to flow to the other, as well as acknowledging the Divinity in the other person. If the Dalai Lama were to bow to you, you would see it as a sign of his great stature, compassion and spiritual humility, not as a sign of weakness. And you would quite appreciate that spirit could flow from him to you.

This aspect of surrender to the other is a beautiful honor offered in grace.

The metaphysical or spiritual aspect of the story would be the interpretation that Lilith wanted to steal Adam's power to add to her own. This, again, is a statement of lack of self-worth. It can sometimes look virtuous as in "stopping the other being so wealthy when many are poor" but it is essentially a belief that there is not enough good, happiness, prosperity or food for every human on earth. Metaphysical teachings follow the rule of cause and effect, and state that we draw to us what we perceive to be the truth. If we try to steal the power (or land or oil) of another, we demonstrate disharmony with ourself and lack of faith in Divine abundance. One of Jesus' most difficult teachings demonstrates this:

> *Unto every one which hath shall be given; and from him that hath not, even that he hath shall be taken away from him.*
> Luke 19:26

It is also common that we give away our power, and then resent the power of the other when they don't do what we want or expect them to do. Giving away power represents laziness and an unwillingness to take responsibility for our own life. We can retain our own power no matter what the other is doing by facing up to our own role in the situation, and recognizing how and why we found ourself in it. To live at this level takes great conscious effort, which is why it is easier to blame others.

A second metaphysical interpretation refers to the androgynous aspect of the Adamah-Lilith created being. This implies that aspects of Adamah refused to bow to other parts of itself. In us, this could refer to our pride being stronger than our desire for spiritual development. So often we don't have the self-discipline to carry out a task which will enhance our life – such as regular meditation, prayer or even promoting our business. So often we eat because we desire the taste of food, not because it is good for us or we are hungry. So this story tells us that if we won't submit to discipline and curb either our lusts, laziness, pride or apathy, part of our psyche will be destructive to our plans (our children). Lilith destroys the offspring of creativity. This is a hard lesson for most of us but perhaps the most powerful one of the inner teachings behind the legend of Lilith.

The mystical aspect of a story is often the simplest one. If Lilith were the breath of God, then the order to Lilith to bow to Adam came from God Itself. This means that God 'spoke' to Lilith *first*. If you want to play the 'I'm most important' game, that makes Lilith number one: the firstborn.

This means it's worth considering that the whole legend might just be about Lilith being unable to receive the light of Divinity and therefore being incapable of passing it on. To bow to Adam would have meant to flow the light to him.

The 'receiving in order to flow onwards' aspect is an important part of the Hebrew Testament laws of tithing. These teach that to prosper, we must first connect with God in order to receive and appreciate His gifts before we give to others.[26]

Had Lilith understood the importance of being chosen as the first to receive the Grace of God before passing it on; had she savored that connection with the Divine, she would happily have listened, received and then passed that heavenly gift onwards to Adam through her bow. She would have known that in doing so, she became Divine herself.

In the legend, she didn't know it. She resented being told what to do and couldn't see that her role in receiving before passing on the light was pivotal to all creation. So her lesson to us is to be willing to receive the Grace and celebrate it so that we can initiate the flow of light throughout humanity instead of seeing the 'other', who has not yet had the knowledge or the opportunity to be filled, as something to criticize or resent.

The revelation is that she made the first error: the assumption that being asked to surrender, she was lesser. This was the first resentment and it has haunted humanity ever since.

In the Four Worlds of Jacob's Ladder Beriah, the World where Lilith was born, is the place of spirit and Air and it flows into Yezirah, the World of forms and Water. Without the Air of spirit, Water will stagnate. Lilith teaches us that unless we will allow the flow of spirit, we cannot grow.

Chapter Six

Cause and Effect – Eve

Name: Eve comes from the Hebrew word *khawah*, 'to breathe' or *khayah*, 'to live'. It is usually translated as 'life'.

Original sin is a Christian concept. Jews and Muslims don't see humanity as needing to be saved. If you haven't sinned, you don't need to be redeemed.

When I was a child, my mother referred to menstruation as 'the curse of Eve'. The concept that women must suffer from being female because we are the cause of the Fall has been endemic for thousands of years.

Perhaps it's time we got over it.

The Hebrew word for sin is *chata* which means 'miss the goal' or 'miss the path'. In Koine (New Testament Greek) it is *hamartia* which means 'to miss the mark' (an archery term) or 'miss the way' or 'to err'.

Eve was the first human being to make a choice and realize that all choices mean consequences. Sometimes we make good choices and sometimes we make what the Buddhists call unskillful ones.

This is how Eve is introduced:

And the Lord God caused a deep sleep to fall upon Adam, and he slept: and he took one of his ribs, and closed up the flesh instead thereof; and the rib, which the Lord God had taken from man, made he a woman, and brought her unto the man. And Adam said, 'This is now bone of my bones, and flesh of my flesh: she shall be called Woman, because she was taken out of Man.'
Genesis 2:21–3

One form of Midrash translates *tsal'ah* (rib) as 'side', as it is the same word used for the phrase "and for the other side wall of the Tabernacle" (Exodus 26:20), equating Eve with the left-hand feminine column of the Tree of Life and perhaps even sanctifying her as daughter of Asherah. Eve is the mother of all creation and the Rabbi authors of Midrash frequently draw parallels between the creation of a family and the erection of the Tabernacle.

Another view from the very same section of Midrash is that Adam and Eve were one androgynous being with joined backs who were split in half[27] creating two soul-mates. Some traditions believe that souls are created with a specific gender; others believe that they are transgender. But the idea of two halves of a whole is a good way of explaining why most humans yearn for a partner. Midrash says that the act of love-making recreates the original perfection that existed during this time of the Creation, so promoting the importance of marriage without which neither man (nor presumably woman) was believed to be complete.[28]

A view that is offered and rejected in the same Genesis Midrash is that Satan was created simultaneously with Eve. This is based on a disputed interpretation that the Hebrew letter *samekh*, which represents 'sin', does not appear from the beginning of Genesis until the creation of Eve. It is disproved but it is still extant in the text and relevant for us here as it adds to the evidence that, for the commentaries, woman was either all virtue or all error. Even without the legend of Lilith, there is enough fuel for demonization. It is not the task of the commentaries to engage with the idea of simple, fallible humanity learning step by step to return to its divine origins. That is our job.

Yet one more rather lovely take on Eve being created from Adam's rib comes from the 18th century Presbyterian minister, Matthew Henry, who said that Eve was not made from Adam's head to top him, nor from his feet to be trampled on by him but from his side to be equal with him, under his arm to be protected by him and near his heart to be loved by him.

The Lord God tells Adam that he can eat from any tree in the garden except the tree of knowledge of good and bad. This is usually translated as 'good and evil' but bad would also be accurate. If either the man or woman in Eden eats from that tree, they will die. When the serpent beguiles Eve to eat the fruit, it says instead that they won't die but will become like gods, in understanding the difference between good and bad. Interestingly, the serpent is described as *aruwm* which means subtle, crafty or sensible. Midrash explains that in contradicting the Lord God, the serpent was the first in creation to speak slander which is why the Israelites were punished by means of serpents when they in turn were slanderous (Numbers 21:6). Even though the Lord God had cursed the serpent, the Israelites did not learn the lesson of its fate.[29]

There is so much Midrash for this story that can easily be found in books and from the Internet, so from here I will work with kabbalistic and original concepts which may provide new food for thought.

The text says that Eve saw that the fruit of the tree was to be desired in order to make her wise (*sakal* – prudent or circumspect) and chose to eat it.

Adam then ate the fruit too and both of them started at once to make choices. They saw that they were naked and believed that this was bad. They didn't have to see it that way but suddenly they had opinions. We still have. Most of the time it is not the event but our opinions about it that make life seem good or bad to us.

But I believe the crux of the story is what happened next. Adam and Eve hid from God because they were naked. God asked them "who told you that you were naked?" and asked if they had eaten from the Tree of Knowledge.

Adam said it was the woman's fault because she gave him the fruit. Then Eve said it was the serpent's fault because it had beguiled her.

That was the beginning of the blame game: the making of the

other person wrong and the denial of self-responsibility. That was the fall; it had nothing to do with the apple. Our time in paradise was over.

Unto Adam also and to his wife did the Lord God make coats of skins, and clothed them. And the Lord God said, Behold, the man is become as one of us, to know good and evil: and now, lest he put forth his hand, and take also of the tree of life, and eat, and live for ever: Therefore the Lord God sent him forth from the garden of Eden, to till the ground from whence he was taken.
Genesis 3:21–3

The Lord God also told them that living outside the Garden of Eden and wearing the coats of skin would hurt.

In Kabbalah, the story of the Tree of Knowledge takes place in the World of *Yezirah*, or Paradise, which is *not* on Earth. So Eden was never a physical place. The man and woman and all the creatures in Eden are formed but not physically born. They are in the World we inhabit before and after death. We all wear coats of skin on Earth but we don't need them in the heavens. And life on Earth does hurt. Mortal bodies have requirements and limitations and they die. So God was right. And yet, so was the serpent: we did become like gods because every decision we make in this world of matter changes and creates things. It's the thought that preempts the reality.

We have to look deeper into the mystical tradition for the essential background to this story and why the move between the psychological World/paradise and physical World needed the Tree of Knowledge and the ability to decide whether a choice was good or bad.

Kabbalah teaches that the whole purpose of creation is for God to be able to experience manifest reality. For that purpose, the Holy One is giving birth to a child that we would call Creation. In the mystical tradition that child is known as Adam

Kadmon – the primordial human being – and it exists in the Divine World of Azilut. Each sentient being in the Universe is one cell in that divine baby and all of us have to become perfect in order for it to be born and for God to be fully manifest in the world. That means that every one of us will, at one point, become enlightened. It may take millennia but that's the plan. Our choices are what will make that destiny easy or terrifying.

Here's a version of the story of the Garden of Eden from the feminine mystery tradition which gives a very beautiful reason for 'the fall'. The author is unknown and the story has been carried through generations by word of mouth.

When the Elohim created the heavens and the Earth She created also the angels and the archangels. She created animals and fish and birds – and man and woman.

They lived in a matchless world; an endless world of perfection and beauty and all was very, very good.

But nothing changed and nothing grew and the soul of Adam Kadmon had no being and was lifeless for it had nothing of its own; nothing that made it unique. Nothing to strive for. Nothing that made it conceive of any moment that could be separate from God where it could make a decision of itself.

For the Elohim did not know how to create separation; all God knew was Absolute and perfect. And so there was a stalemate.

Then, one day, as the Elohim passed over the waters of the Earth that She had created to be the growing place of the baby when it had quickened, something caught the Holy One's attention. It was an oyster, with its shell open on the sands at the bottom of the sea. But it was not the oyster itself that drew the Holy One; it was the pearl within it; silver and purple and milky and shining and smooth.

The Elohim spoke to the oyster who carried this pearl and said: "O Oyster, I give you the greetings of this perfect day and I beg you to tell me, what is that which is inside your shell? For I know that I made you and for certain, I did not make that."

And the oyster looked at the Elohim and said, humbly, "My Mother and my Delight, it is a pearl that I made myself. I hope that it does not displease you."

"Displease me?" said the Elohim in surprise. "How could anything displease me? All that is, is of me and all of me is perfection. But how come you created this pearl, O Oyster? I have seen no angel, nor archangel, nor animal, nor fish, nor bird, nor human create in this world of paradise but you."

"My Mother and my Delight," said the oyster. "I opened my shell to drink and a grain of dust – of perfect dust – flowed in with the water. And it caused me to be uncomfortable.

"I tried to expel it but I could not do so. So I covered it with a part of myself to make it smooth and comfortable instead of irritating. Now I take pleasure in it instead of pain. Is it not beautiful?"

"Beautiful?" said the Elohim. "It is more than beautiful. It is the most wonderful thing that I have ever seen. Thank you, O Oyster, you are my teacher and I am truly grateful."

Then the Holy One spent time in contemplation, for the new knowledge that the oyster had given was a treasure which required full enjoyment. And then, the Elohim made a decision and knew that it was very good.

The Elohim moved to the place where the man and the woman lived in peace and harmony with themselves and with the creatures and She called them and He spoke to them.

"The greetings of this perfect day to you," She said. "I have something to tell you. Do you see that tree over there?"

The man and the woman greeted the Holy One in turn, and in great happiness, and they looked and surely enough there was a tree – a great tree – which they had not seen before. It was tall and elegant and it carried luscious-looking fruits. They laughed for they had great joy in anticipation and they knew how much they would enjoy those fruits.

"You are not to eat of the tree," said Yahweh Elohim. "You may

66

look at it and enjoy it but you are not to eat from it. Not one fruit. Never."

Now the man and the woman had not heard such a command before. All the Elohim's words had been "yes" to them. They did not understand.

And the Elohim's heart melted with compassion for Her creations for She saw that they experienced distress at His command. But the Holy One also knew, with the greatest of joy, that what the oyster had taught was true.

"You can do anything else," said the Holy One. "Anything. But do not eat of that tree."

And then Yahweh Elohim left the man and the woman alone with the tiny grain of sand that He had slipped inside their minds and waited patiently for the moment that they decided to act to create their own lives.

The Elohim knew immediately that it happened; for Adam Kadmon's soul quickened and life surged into it. The Divine Child began to grow at last.

But the Holy One also knew that every cell in Adam Kadmon would have to know of grit for the baby to thrive so Yahweh steeled the Elohim's heart and returned to see the humans and told them that it was now time for them to leave the world of paradise and to be born into a lower world of physical life and death. There, they would have to make choices every moment of every day and, through their choices, they would become unique and different. And their belief in their separation from God would cause them to choose always whether to seek the Holy One or to turn away.

As they left the Garden to take on their coats of skin and live in the physical world as we do now, Eve was carrying a twig from that wonderful tree in her hand. It was a piece of twig that came off when she pulled at the fruit and it had a couple of leaves on it.

And as she left, she bent down and planted that twig in the ground so that it would grow, tall and mighty, becoming a Way that could show all of humanity the way back home.

Eve and the Tree of Life

All known kabbalistic traditions place Eve at the sefira of *Binah* which means Understanding. The *Talmud Niddah* 45b says that "the Lord fashioned (*va-yiven*) the rib" from which Eve was created which is directly linked with the Hebrew "*bina yetera*" meaning that God gave greater powers of understanding, insight and intuitive intelligence to woman than to man.

Binah is at the head of the feminine pillar of the Tree of Life and is associated with Karma, cause and effect, boundaries and law. Binah is the Great Mother, the Great Sea, paralleled with the Elohim: the archetypal womb from which all life comes into manifestation.

However, she also represents restriction, binding and limitation which is why the left-hand column is also known as the Pillar of Severity. The right-hand column is also known as the Pillar of Mercy and many may think that motherhood is more on the merciful side. However, it is the traditional mother's role to teach the rules of life from "don't touch that, it's hot" to "look both ways before you cross the road." And as the Great Mother gives birth, she also understands that birth will always result in death. This is the first and great lesson of cause and effect.

Binah is often called the Dark Mother and is the aspect of the feminine which is associated with suffering. She is equated to the *Mater Dolorosa* – Our Lady of Sorrows – the statues of the Virgin Mary where she is weeping. In Christian Kabbalah, Mary is also placed at Binah as the transformation of the sin of Eve.

Whether or not Eve sinned in the Garden of Eden, she is the source of all life and consequently the source of all death, grief and suffering. The Dark Mother understands this and holds a space for us to heal within that knowledge.

Levels of Interpretation

Literally and allegorically, Eve's story is simple; you make a choice and you get a consequence. Consequences cannot always be anticipated because we do not understand the story or the agenda of the others involved.

Every one of us has found life unfair at times and chosen to see it as the fault of 'the other' as we only did what they expected or told us to do. But all spiritual teachings are about taking one hundred percent responsibility for our actions, and it is important to realize that even *not* choosing to make a conscious decision is a decision in itself. We are not responsible for our actions if we are not willing to be conscious beings, but we are if we choose to step up and even begin to call ourselves spiritual.

Eve's story may touch you in a way that is deeply personal, whether it was a deep inner feeling that the feminine or women are unequal to the masculine or men or, that women suffer because they disobeyed God. These views can affect a whole life if they are not brought to consciousness and addressed.

The mystical view is that there was no 'fall', just a chance to experience the pattern of choice and consequence which affects every living being. As humans, we have to learn from our choices in order to create and maintain a sustainable society. Have we done it? The matter is still in question.

The translation of the Ultimate Name of God – 'I Will Be That Which I Will Be' – implies that the Divine and the Universe will appear to us exactly as we appear to them. If we are judgmental, angry, blaming, then God and life will appear to us to be the same. If we are loving, kind and generous, then God and life will appear to us to be the same. This is all about our use of free will. In Adam and Eve's story, they blamed – and therefore God appeared to blame them with the curses of hard work and pain in the physical World. These are only curses if seen from the negative view. To those of us who live on Earth, toil and pain are simple realities. It is what it is – and our consciousness affects every aspect of how we experience it, and the choices that we make in consequence.

Part Three

Living in the Tribe

Chapter Seven

The Matriarchs

There are four 'Matriarchs' of the Hebrew Testament: Sarah, Rebekah, Leah and Rachel. On the surface, it would appear that their entire relevance is through their husbands and children. This, kabbalistically, would be quite appropriate because these four women are placed on the bottom four sefirot of the Tree of Life (fig. 4).

This triad of Common Humanity is the area which reflects tribal and family life. It's sometimes known as the Vegetable Triad. That isn't intended to be rude, just realistic. We all have vegetable, animal and human characteristics and the vegetable part of us is just as important as the other two.

This triad reflects the part of our psyche which is predicated on survival, food, sexuality and reproduction. These are the characteristics of plants rather than animals. They also push their way through to the sunlight even if it means climbing over others to get there.

The Uncommon Humanity or Animal Level of us competes, hunts, nurtures, individuates, plays, remembers, shares, takes a stand, fights, leads or follows, forms things from existing materials and educates. All of these require a little more effort, but are often very closely linked with the vegetable level.

In Kabbalah, the goal for all humanity is to merge these two levels with the additional aspect of our soul's purpose – the level of true humanity: that of Heroes and Heroines. This level is where we become conscious instead of acting on instinct or adrenaline. Here we imagine, create, laugh, connect with all humanity and with our Higher Self. We gaze in wonder at the world and the starlit heavens and ponder the meaning of life. At this level we are no longer concerned with the tribe but with the path and meaning of spiritual evolution. We can see the wider picture rather than just what is in front of our face.

We all know how good it is to 'veg out' with a takeaway and a DVD on an evening when we are tired. Those of us who have children know what a miracle parenthood is, and anyone who's ever felt the pull of desire when meeting someone new won't have any problem with the excitement of the vegetable level. Vegetable stuff is fun and relevant, and vital to our happiness.

The only way that this level within us becomes negative is when it rules the whole of our life. It can come to do so when we don't make our own conscious choices or wake up to possibilities outside the tribal beliefs. In the modern world these tribal beliefs include what we are told on the news or in our favorite magazines. It's easier to believe them and to hand out blame than it is to step away and see situations with clarity. It becomes destructive when we don't meld this level with our animal and human selves, and learn to balance our own desires and our relationship with the Divine with the pull of family needs. Depression is often a result of living a negatively vegetable life; the person feels that they have no intrinsic value in themselves, that they are not known, recognized or wanted for who they really are, but only as an adjunct to someone else's life.

Vegetable/tribal belief in Biblical days was that women belonged to their fathers or husbands and that any property or dowry they brought with them would belong to the man although it could become theirs at his death or on divorce. It was vital that they were a virgin when they married – and they could be divorced immediately if they were discovered not to be – and they also faced the possibility of divorce if they were infertile. A kinder alternative, when a wife who was loved did not produce children, was polygamy. While this was not necessarily encouraged, it was seen as preferable to childlessness, as we will see from many of the stories.

Giving birth only to daughters could also be seen as infertility.

Male heirs were essential to carry on the tribe by being able to work, trade, fight and protect the women, the young and the weak. It's easy to object to the way things were viewed then but it is most likely that women in those days did not have any of the emotions about it that the modern-day self-sufficient, independent working woman might have.

As a young woman was married within six months of her first menses, she would most likely have her first baby before the age of 14 and, no matter how much we like to think that the women were oppressed, most of the privileges we take for granted simply weren't an option if your life was filled with pregnancy, miscarriage, perinatal death and the need either to farm or find food to sustain the tribe when the hunt did not bring back enough.

The warrior-like heroines who crop up in modern films depicting ancient days were certainly the exception rather than the rule. It's interesting that the heroines of the Hebrew Testament are less revered than the Matriarchs – but their stories appear outside the Torah which is regarded as the heart of Judaism.

The vegetable level is strongly linked to the level of the psyche known in Kabbalah as *Yesod*. This is our foundation: the part of us that our true self relies on to support us in our growth. It is also known as ego, and this is the part of our psyche which likes to maintain the status quo and keep us in the position that the tribe requires us to hold. If we do that, then we will be safe – and the ego's primary function is to keep us alive.

There is a Jesuit saying, "Give me the child until he is seven and I will give you the man" which perfectly describes Yesod. From birth to around that time, our egos are all malleable and will form in whatever way is required to keep us safe and supported in the tribe. A human child needs nurturing and guidance as well as food, and the ego will ensure that it behaves in a way that will get the attention that is needed. For some this means compliance with rules, and for others it means rebellion in order to stick out.

When we come from ego we are always feeling either inferior or superior to others, and we are always assessing them as being either on our side or opposing us. This is an automatic judgment system of what is right or wrong that is developed from our genes and our training.

In Kabbalah, this part of the primal nature of the psyche is represented by one's astrological Moon sign. Whether you believe in astrology or not, it's important to realize that in Biblical times, people did. In Biblical times astronomers were always looking for signs and portents in the skies. The wise men who visited the baby Jesus were *Magi* which means 'astrologer priests'.

It is only the modern, scientific world that regards techniques that require belief in more than the five senses as being irrelevant or incorrect. It is part of humanity's psyche at the moment to debunk the spiritual or unseen, but it is a good example of the ego's arrogance to assume that all that we humans can perceive is all that is manifestly real. In fact we can perceive less than one percent of either the color or sound spectra that surround us.

However, in ancient days, birth charts were rare. Unless it was the birth of a prince, most people didn't keep note of the day and time that they were born. Instead they went to astrologers to cast charts for future events to see what outcome was likely if a project was begun on a certain day, and asked specific questions about life based on the timing of the query. William Lilly (1602–1681) wrote what is viewed as the classic text on what has come to be known as 'Horary Astrology'.[30] Lilly predicted the Great Fire of London fourteen years before its occurrence and, for that, was tried by Parliament, accused of having started it. He was acquitted.

Astrology was always seen as what happens when we don't use free will rather than events set in stone. It's the diagram of how the vegetable and animal levels work on automatic if we don't think clearly. When we operate on the human or conscious level we can rise above our astrology or any other system such as Human Design, the Enneagram, Feng Shui or Biorhythms.

So, the stories of the Matriarchs are about women who are acting from the everyday level of survival. This is not to insult them. These are the first women recorded to have lived on Earth, therefore they are young souls, probably here for the first time. Kabbalah teaches that the human soul reincarnates in order to undertake four journeys. The first is the descent from Paradise to learn how to live in the physical World. The second is learning how to develop the psyche and soul. The third is to assist others to learn – and is often attained in conjunction with the second in that we learn a little and teach a little and then learn a little more. The fourth journey is the return to the heavens as a fully-realized human being.

There is a school of thought that not all human souls are incarnate as yet, and that it is becoming increasingly difficult for new souls to learn in the first journey as they are mostly, nowadays, born into cities. The first journey is far more easily undertaken in so-called primitive societies where there is a strong and healthy *Yesod* of a tribe. Then the first journey can be assimilated while learning survival skills, farming, hunting and socialization in a small community of like-minded people. In cities, our relationships and our communities are often fractured and, in the Western world, children do not grow up in extended families with mutual beliefs and support. American mystic, Joseph Campbell, taught that when young men steal a car and burn it on a Saturday night they are trying to "kill their lion"[31] – to undertake a tribal ritual of manhood which, in the savannahs or forests, would have been an important ceremony of passage involving training, discipline and commitment.

The Matriarchs are all revered within Judaism and rightly so considering the youth of their souls and the challenging aspects of life that they have to deal with. It is clear as we move on to the later stories of the women that, once they rise above the tribal level, they can stand on the knowledge their ancestors taught them. Their mistakes become fewer and their lives become clearer.

Even so, there is a lot that the Matriarchs can teach us. Just like us, their entire lives were directed by their choices and also by their decisions not to choose. Choosing not to choose is a choice in itself.

Chapter Eight

Survival of the Fittest – Sarah and Hagar

Names: Sarai in Hebrew means 'princess' and Sarah means 'noblewoman'.

Hagar has several different translations, notably 'stranger' and 'flight'. The latter is from the Arabic word *hegira*. Hagar is said to be of Arabic/Egyptian origin. The word is not used anywhere else in the Bible and is not a Hebraic noun. Midrash says that *Ha-Agar* means 'this is the reward'.

In the women's stories, Sarah is called "the Mother of all Israel" whereas Eve is "the Mother of all Creation".

The mother is the one who gives life and yet Sarah is best known for her barrenness (Genesis 11:30). She had one, late-born son Isaac who was conceived after the menopause (Genesis 18:11). It is worth noting that only three of the four Matriarchs found it easy to conceive and the one who was abundantly fertile was known as 'the unloved'.

With Sarah's story we begin life after 'the fall'. We drop from the Supernal Triad of the Tree of Life, which has direct contact with the Source, to the very base of the structure to begin the pathway back to the Divine. Sarah is down and dirty in the world of reality. Although I will refer to Midrash wherever it is relevant to the story from now on, I believe that its tendency to excuse traits such as jealousy, revenge, resentment and depression, seeking only the perfect in the Matriarchs, is counterproductive. You can't find the Divine Feminine in continual justification and praise; the Dark Mother, the bitterness and the pain have to be acknowledged, too, and the journey of the women through the trials of everyday life are much more relevant to us than paeans of praise for paragons of virtue to whom we could never aspire.

Sarah's story is inseparable from Hagar's, and this begins a pattern where two women are working together at the soul level to fulfill the story.

Sarah and Hagar's lives are intertwined through their relationship with Abraham, and through their children Isaac and Ishmael. In the Hebrew Testament, it is Isaac who is taken for sacrifice by Abraham and saved by Divine intervention on Mount Moriah; in the Islamic tradition, though the Qur'an does not actually state which son it is, it is typically believed that Abraham is told to sacrifice the eldest, Ishmael, not Isaac. This disagreement as to which son was the most important and most loved has colored Arab-Israeli relations ever since. If Sarah and Hagar could have worked together at a spiritual or soul level, this conflict might never have started. That is how powerful these two women were and still are today.

The commentaries all honor Sarah highly. The *Zohar* says that Eve was tempted by the serpent and fell whereas Sarah fell down but came up again and never attached herself to the serpent. I think that view can be challenged as Sarah's life was almost devoured by the serpent of envy.

Sarah's place on the Tree of Life is at Malkhut, the sefira of physical manifestation and survival. Malkhut means *kingdom* and Sarah is the royal mother of the entire Hebrew line. Her life is both magical and mundane, filled with the Grace of God and the curse of jealousy.

Hagar is placed in the right-hand triad touching Malkhut. It is important that she should be strongly linked with this sefira for her son began the Arabic nation. Although her name means 'stranger' in Hebrew and she is an Egyptian, the *Zohar* says that Hagar was Pharaoh's daughter. This makes her, too, a princess though not of the Hebrew line. If it is so, then she went from royalty to slavery and then to willfulness and exile.

Sarah is originally named Sarai and her husband is Abram. We know nothing of her life before she marries although the Bible says (Genesis 20:12) that she is also Abram's half-sister – marriage was permitted, in those days, between children of the same father though not of the same mother. We also know, from the very first mention in Genesis 11:30, that Sarai is barren.

Abram and Sarai came from Ur of the Chaldees (now in Iraq) and they are revered throughout Judaism and Islam for worshipping the one God in a polytheistic area.

The Lord tells Abram that he must leave his home country and his family, continuing the tradition of exile which began with Adam and Eve. Very few of the great souls of the Hebrew Testament lived a life safely at home.

"I will make of thee a great nation and I will bless thee and make thy name great," says the Lord (Genesis 12:1). However, it's clear from the Hebrew at this point that He is only addressing Abram and not Sarai.

They go to live in Shechem in Canaan, where Abram builds an altar to the Lord, but there is a famine in the land and Abram decides to move further south to find a place which is more comfortable to live.

The Lord had not told them to go to Egypt and, the *Zohar* says, this was tantamount to disobedience. In Kabbalah the word 'Egypt' represents a place where people are enslaved by their desires and thoughts and, as Abram and Sarai go into Egypt, Abram becomes afraid of his wife's beauty, believing it may be a threat to his safety. He thinks that Pharaoh will want to have Sarai as his mistress and will kill Abram to make it so. So Abram tells Sarai to say that she is his sister but not his wife, so that he will be safe.

The *Zohar* explains Abram's request away by saying that by calling Sarai his sister, Abram was acknowledging the Shekhinah in her and that, whatever happened, she would be safe. This sounds like justification after the event and even appears to contradict the *Zohar's* own teaching about Shekhinah and marriage.

It's not clear what Sarai thinks of Abram's request but she obeys it. Because Pharaoh admires Sarai so much, he does take her into his harem and, in return for her, he gives Abram sheep, oxen, asses, camels and slaves. This may have been when Hagar joined Abram's tribe. The Biblical Hebrew makes it quite clear that Pharaoh never had sex with Sarai, and that God sent plagues to make him and his family utterly miserable. Midrash adds that Sarai pleaded with God and God sent an angel with a whip to strike Pharaoh any time he tried to molest her.

All that night the angel stood there with the whip. If Sarai bade him 'Strike,' he would strike him. If she told him, 'Cease,' he ceased. Even though Sarai told Pharaoh: 'I am a married woman,' he did not desist from his efforts to touch her.[32]

Not surprisingly, Pharaoh wonders why this is all happening and Sarai must have told him the truth because he goes to Abram and says words to the effect of: "Why on earth did you not tell me that your sister was your wife?"

It turns out that Pharaoh is more than a fair man and he is horrified that he might have done something wrong with Sarai, and he lets her go immediately and suggests (very politely, considering what he has had to go through) that they make their way out of Egypt while keeping all the goods that he has given to Abram. It's interesting how often, in the Hebrew Testament, it is the outsiders who behave with the greatest honor. I believe that there must be a message for us in that. However, it is not the view taken in the commentaries.

Abram and Sarai settle again in the land of Canaan, and Abram (and possibly Sarai) receives an initiation through an encounter with a mystical priest, Melchizedek, King of Salem. The *Zohar* says that Melchizedek means 'king of righteousness' and Salem means 'completeness' (Jerusalem means 'he shall see completeness').

Melchizedek is credited with being a manifestation of the great Archangel Metatron who is the only known being which is both angel and human and was once Enoch. Kabbalah teaches that Metatron will manifest in the world whenever a great teaching needs to be renewed. It's said that he came down to Earth to tell Abram about the *Book of Raziel* which was given to Adam and Eve after they left the Garden of Eden. This shows the way back from everyday life to Paradise, and it still exists today in the kabbalistic teaching and, in the modern world, in many spiritual traditions.

In Genesis, Melchizedek brought bread and wine. A bread and wine sacrifice became an integral part of the First Temple (animal sacrifice began with the Second Temple in about 500 BCE although there is evidence of human sacrifice before then). This is possibly similar to the ceremony Jesus uses at the Last Supper. In the *Book of Hebrews* in the New Testament, Jesus is referred to as a priest after the order of Melchizedek.

By now Abram and Sarai have been married for many years but they do not have any children despite the fact that the Lord has told Abram for the second time that he was to be the father of a new nation.

Sarai obviously considers the matter long and hard and she believes that her barrenness is irreversible. "Behold now, the Lord hath restrained me from bearing" (Genesis 16:2). Midrash, in the episode with Pharaoh, implies that Sarai can communicate with the Lord but this is not evident from the Biblical text; she appears there to have very little faith at all.

Instead, Sarai offers Abram her servant Hagar so that he can become a father and fulfill the prophecy. Being a slave, Hagar wouldn't have had any say in the matter; she belonged body and soul to her mistress. Islam says that Hagar became Abram's second wife but the Hebrew word used, *ishsha*, could mean either woman or wife.

Abram accepts Sarai's offer and Hagar becomes pregnant.

The Rabbis in the Midrash had a real problem over how Sarai the princess did not conceive from Abram while Hagar the foreigner and slave became pregnant immediately. They explained that Hagar gave birth to Ishmael with such ease because he was like "worthless thorns", in contrast to Sarai's future birth of Isaac, who was the true son. Sarai's difficulty in conceiving, therefore, was due to the quality of the child she would produce.[33]

Hopefully this kind of interpretation is unacceptable to most of us today even without modern medical knowledge of fertility levels and issues.

Sarai would have expected Hagar's child to be the nearest thing to her own son – as child of her slave he would be her property. But the pregnant Hagar makes it very plain that her star is in the ascendant and that she despises Sarai for not being able to have children herself. As she is now going to be the mother of Abram's son, she believes she can be as rude as she liked.

Sarai complains bitterly to Abram:

My wrong be upon thee: I have given my maid into thy bosom; and when she saw that she had conceived, I was despised in her eyes: the Lord judge between me and thee.
Genesis 16:50

Abram obviously loves and respects his wife deeply. He could easily have chosen the pregnant Hagar, who was fulfilling the Lord's promise to him that he would father a nation, over the barren, hostile wife. But he tells Sarai that Hagar is her servant and it is up to her to decide what to do. Sarai promptly starts being so mean to her slave that Hagar runs away into the desert – to almost certain death.

Hagar must have been terrified. Genesis says that God sends an angel to her to say that she'd better go back and submit. The angel finds her by a fountain of water – the first of a line of links between the women of the Hebrew Testament and living water (Genesis 16:7). It also tells her that, although her son would be a quarrelsome man, he would have many descendants so that she would become the mother of a nation. News like that, and the knowledge that your prayers were heard, might make it easier to swallow your pride.

Once the angel has left, Hagar goes back home. She must have had to apologize to Sarai, which would have been hard, and the relationship between the two women is always hostile, as it so often is between first and second wife in a modern marriage. Just because Sarai was still Abram's wife didn't mean that she felt secure. And it must have been a mixed joy and bitterness when Hagar gives birth to a healthy boy child and Sarai sees Abram rejoice.

Thirteen years pass and the Lord comes again to Abram, calling himself by a new name: *El Shaddai* the Living Almighty God. Something has changed as *El Shaddai* says, "walk before me, and be thou perfect" (Genesis 17:1) and tells Abram that there should be a covenant between them and, as a symbol of it, both he and his wife should be renamed Abraham and Sarah. Abraham's family is to be circumcised and, in return, Sarah will give birth to a son. This was the "great covenant" which has led to all orthodox Jewish men being circumcised ever since.

Abraham does all that God, now returning to the name *Elohim*, asks and once it is completed the Lord visits and speaks to him in the form of three angels. One angel tells Abraham that Sarah will bear a son. Sarah is listening at the tent door and she laughs at the very idea. The Lord asks Abraham why she is laughing and Sarah denies it. The English translation says: *"And he said, Nay; but thou didst laugh"* (Genesis 18:15). The implication is that it is Abraham speaking but Midrash is clear that it is the Lord and that Sarah is the only woman with whom He converses directly in the Hebrew Testament.[34] This is either forgetting Eve or an acknowledgment that Eve was not an incarnate human being in the Garden of Eden.

It is interesting that this seminal contact involves a lie from

Sarah: a denial, a defense, quite similar to that of Eve.

Truth is the issue in the next strand of the story, too. After the destruction of the towns of Sodom and Gomorrah, Sarah and Abraham travel again. In the southern land of Gerar, the king, Abimelech, admires Sarah. Abraham says, a second time, that she is his sister so that the King will not kill him in order to have her himself. Why does this story happen again? This indicates the law of Karma – that if we don't learn our lessons the first time, then the same will happen again. Sarah backs Abraham up again and Abimelech takes her for his wife.

Perish the thought but did Abraham know what would happen; that the Shekhinah would save Sarah again and he would end up with extra livestock or treasures? That's exactly what happened, a second time.

Instead of sending plagues, God (rather than the Lord) appears to Abimelech and tells him that Sarah is Abraham's wife. Abimelech is horrified, calls Abraham, restores Sarah to him and asks him why he had set him up to commit such a great sin. Abraham says "but she is my half-sister" and Abimelech sends him away with cattle and servants. Again, it would appear that the person outside the tribe has behaved in the more honorable way whereas the hero and heroine have used deceit. However, when the Lord causes Abimelech and his family to become barren because he took Sarah, Abraham shows mercy in praying to God for them to be healed, which they are.

After this, Sarah conceives. That this is a miracle baby and not just a natural happening is emphasized: *"And the Lord visited Sarah as he had said, and the Lord did unto Sarah as he had spoken"* (Genesis 21:1). She gives birth to a healthy son, Isaac, which means 'laughter' in Hebrew.

After the longed-for child is born Sarah says,

God has made laughter for me; everyone who hears will laugh on account of me. Who would have said unto Abraham that Sarah

should give children suck? For I have borne him a son in his old age.
Genesis 21:6–7

Midrash carefully addresses two possible issues here: the first being to make it clear that Sarah's miracle child is not the son of Abimelech, and the second refuting an apparent accusation that Sarah, being past menopause, does *not* give birth to Isaac, merely pretends that she does. It also relates that when Sarah became pregnant, all the barren women of the world became pregnant, all the deaf became capable of hearing, all the blind were given sight, all the mutes were cured and all the madmen became sound of mind.[35] Simultaneously it says that all women who have given birth failed to be able to offer milk and that Sarah suckles the children of the world, thereby showing that she had, herself, given birth.[36]

This is most likely to be symbolic of the birth of Isaac and the new nation of Israel that Abraham and Sarah had founded providing new life for the world.

Sarah and Hagar are obviously still wary of each other and, when Isaac is weaned at about the age of three (there was a special feast in those days for the weaning of a child), Sarah sees Ishmael mocking her son. She goes to Abraham and says, *"Cast out this bondwoman and her son; for the son of this bondwoman shall not be heir with my son"* (Genesis 21:10).

That must have been hard for Abraham, because he loved Ishmael, but God tells him to listen to Sarah because Isaac was destined to be Abraham's heir. Ishmael was to found his own nation.

Abraham gives Hagar and Ishmael food and water and sends them away. And here, there is an interesting clue to the ages in this part of Genesis. Sarah is said to be 90 years old when she bore Isaac, and Ishmael is said to be thirteen when Isaac is born. It is another three years until Hagar and Ishmael are sent away and yet, when the food and water run out in the desert, Hagar "cast the child under the shrubs" (Genesis 21:15) so that she will not have to see him die. A strapping fifteen-year-old would not be regarded as a child or submit to being placed under a bush by his mother. If we are to take these stories literally, the only feasible answer would be that we are to see the years in Genesis as being six months long. Sarah at 45 would, in those days, be past menopause but still possibly capable of conceiving and the Ishmael cast under the bush, aged seven or eight.

The Bible says that, through an angel, God (not the Lord) opens Hagar's eyes so that she can see that she is right next to a well or spring of water (Genesis 21:19). From then onwards, God is with Ishmael and he becomes the father of the Arab nation. This is the first association we have with the women of the Hebrew Testament and the living water of Wisdom. At what level did the angel open Hagar's eyes? Perhaps she perceived that she was the author of her own problems and would become a wiser woman in her new life.

Sarah is excluded from the next big story, where Abraham is told to sacrifice Isaac to God and, at the last minute, is given a ram instead, so we have no idea if she ever even knew of the plan. We could say that, if they trusted God's word that Isaac was the start of a new nation, he could not die before he had fathered children so this is seen to be a test of Abraham's faith. Certainly, sacrifice of the firstborn son was observed in many cultures in those ancient days and the law in Leviticus 20:2–5 forbidding it is seen to be a reaction to an earlier practice.

Many more things happen to Isaac and to Abraham but what Sarah thinks about those nobody knows for she is not mentioned again until her death at the age of 127. Abraham and Isaac mourn for her greatly and the account of her burial is the first story in the Bible about how the Hebrews honored their dead.

Sarah, Hagar and the Tree of Life

Sarah and her story are placed at Malkhut, the sefira of manifestation. All that God has created is made evident at Malkhut. It is also the place of survival, propagation and kingship. Sarah's story tells of all three of these – she and Abraham do whatever they can to survive in what they believe to be hostile foreign lands, they are princes of all they survey: *"Abram was very rich in cattle, in silver, and in gold"* (Genesis 31:12) and they are the parents of the whole Israelite line.

Hagar, too, is a woman of Malkhut but her place is in the triad between Malkhut, Nezah and Yesod which is known as the Triad of Willfulness. This represents the aspect of the survival instinct and the ego which focuses on arrogance, demanding its own way without consideration of the feelings of others. This tendency can often have the reverse affect of the one intended. Hagar's survival comes into question twice when she first runs away and then is sent away for allowing her son to be arrogant.

Malkhut is the mother of us all. A baby in the uterus is said to grow from Keter to Malkhut. The Divine spark comes from Keter, the conception through Hokhmah, the lodging in the womb at Binah and the possibility of spontaneous abortion at Daat (this is known as the non-sefira which is the window between Worlds on the invisible path between Binah and Hesed).

At Hesed, the fetus begins to grow, at Gevurah the bones and organs are formed, at Tiferet, the first stirrings of life and movement can be detected, at Nezah the baby grows again, at Hod the organs of elimination are finalized, at Yesod the baby turns for presentation to the vagina and at Malkhut the child is born.

At Malkhut we focus on the basics in life. Every soul is born to Malkhut and grows to maturity stretching up the Tree of Life, learning the skills of living along the way. Midrash aside, neither Sarah nor Hagar live in the comfort of security. In dire circumstances, both are helped by direct Divine intervention. The Shekhinah, the presence of God, directly associated with the sefira of Malkhut in the Divine World, interposes either directly or through the offices of an angel.

Levels of Interpretation

What is the story of Sarah and Hagar to us today? At the literal level it tells of how two women who could have worked together to raise two sons to be friends decide, instead, to be enemies. It's a tale as old as the hills and in the 21st century it happens as frequently as ever. The only difference for us is that, in the Western world, we divorce and marry again instead of being polygamous. But the rivalry between women who have shared a man can still be vicious. It is a survival trait – my child must be the favored one; it is a tribal attribute – my child is the heir. But it is a tragic one as well. If it is true that Isaac is the founder of the Jewish nation and Ishmael the founder of the Arabic one, then perhaps these brothers' constant warring today dates back to the original mothers' inability to get on together and make peace. And it is worth considering how, in the 21st century, women could work together to create peace in the Middle East and other war-torn areas (and in families too). This is not a new idea but it is a powerful one.

Aristophanes' play *Lysistrata*, first performed in Athens in 411 BCE, tells of how the women of Greece withheld sex from their men in order to make them end the Peloponnesian War between Athens and Sparta. Here, too, it is the women fighting amongst themselves that makes Lysistrata's plan so hard to carry out but it works in the end.

All too often, it is women hailing husbands and sons (and nowadays even daughters) as heroes for going to war and killing others which leads to the idea that war is still, somehow, honorable instead of a political killing machine. From Sarah and Hagar to the present day, the women are the ones with the power to say "enough". Why do we not do so when it is our children who are killed? The answer is in the loyalty to the tribe and the fear that another tribe might rule us. It is a sad answer but nonetheless a powerful and realistic one.

At the allegorical level, the stories of Sarah and Hagar tell us that we repeat patterns without perhaps realizing it. Hagar is exiled for the second time after Sarah sees Ishmael mocking Isaac at his weaning. Ishmael would not have done so unless he had learnt that this was acceptable behavior and his father would never have taught him that. So Hagar was the instrument of her own banishment.

Sarah also repeated the same pattern of allowing Abraham to deny that she was his wife. Admittedly, women were the possessions of their men in those days but it had already been shown that Sarah was an honored and respected wife. It is rarely easy to stand up to speak a truth when it means contradicting someone we love. Self-esteem is still seen as arrogance by many but it is indicated that both Pharaoh and Abimelech were honorable men and, if Sarah had said "no" to Abraham and insisted that he said she was his wife, neither of them would have been harmed.

Of course there were other kings who might not have been honorable, but this is a couple who were in direct contact with the Lord; who had the ability to listen to His word and who were promised that they would be founders of a nation. If Abraham believed the Lord's word at all, he would have known that he was not going to be killed. A fair-weather faith is no faith at all and yet it is the faith that most people experience at the tribal level where the external world appears to be stronger than God's power. A deeper level of faith, from the soul, will stand up for truth and kindness.

At the metaphysical level, the story will either speak to our soul's journey or not. This level is the spiritual one – and the dichotomy within it is that although it is *our* story it is not an individual one because our thoughts and behavior affect the whole world. So working out whether the story attracts or repels us will tell us much about our own self, working at the tribal level. Do we hold hatreds towards others who challenge us? At the spiritual level, we *are* capable of working on forgiveness and love. We just have to apply the self-discipline to work out how and do the work.

At the mystical level, this is a story about young souls. They are making the basic mistakes that all people existing at the survival and tribal levels make. All is perfectly natural and understandable. Sarah and Hagar's stories provide a foundation for the later women to build on. They can learn from their ancestors' mistakes – or not.

Chapter Nine

Taking Control – Rebekah

Name: Rebekah comes from the Hebrew *ribqah*, 'to tie firmly' or 'to secure'. This is a verb that is not used elsewhere in the Bible but equivalent languages have it, so it is assumed that it was also used by the Israelites.

Rebekah's story is all about family and our place in the tribe. Even today, phrases such as "family comes first" are seen as evidence of good behavior and, in a tribal situation, this is true. Living by the rules is the glue that holds society together. But we are looking at the holy text of the Bible where family lore is our foundation but not necessarily part of our spiritual path. In fact, holding on to tribal rulings can be harmful and most spiritual seekers are fringe-dwellers who move away from the tribe. Joseph Campbell spoke and wrote of "the Hero's Journey" where the aspirant has to leave and experience adventure, trial and tribulation before he or she can return to the tribe transformed as an example to others.

With Rebekah's story we clearly see the workings of Karma, or cause and effect. Most people tend to think of Karma as being a bad thing but it is simply the return of the energy we or our families have put out. As Sir Isaac Newton's third law of motion decrees: "for every action, there is an equal and opposite reaction." There is plenty of good Karma in the world as well as bad.

Energy can neither be built nor destroyed; it can only change form. The spiritual dimension adds a rider; that when we have something to learn from Karma, for whatever reason, situations will repeat themselves until we have understood.

The Second Commandment refers to Karma when it says: "I, the Lord thy God, am a jealous god, visiting the iniquity of the fathers upon the children unto the third and fourth ... of them that hate me." Usually, where the dots are, the word 'generation' is inserted in English but it doesn't exist in the Hebrew. It *could* mean 'incarnation' and the 'children' could refer to either the descendants of the perpetrator, or himself or herself returned in all innocence for a new incarnation.

There is plenty of both good and bad Karma in Rebekah's story.

Rebekah is the wife of Isaac, Abraham and Sarah's son. Abraham sends his steward to find and bring back a suitable girl from their own blood to be Isaac's wife. This is most likely to have been Eliezer, the man named in Genesis 15:2 as Abraham's heir if he had no children.

Eliezer travels to Nahor in the country of Mesopotamia where Abraham has relatives. He has to find a girl of the right age and caste so he sits by a well – a spring of water – and prays that he will know the girl when she comes to fetch water by the fact that she will offer him a drink and then to raise water for his camels. That would denote tenderness of heart and kindness to animals. In the Talmud it says that no one should sit down to eat before they have fed their animals.[37] However, the Hidden Tradition is also showing its face here: Eliezer is seeking a woman who has the spiritual grace of wisdom.

It happens just as he asked, for the very first girl he sees offers him water, and also water for his camels, and turns out to be Rebekah who is a cousin of Isaac's. She also has the advantages of being beautiful of face and the right, marriageable age. Eliezer has brought gifts for Isaac's future bride and he gives her a golden nose ring (most translations say 'earring' because for many generations nose rings have not been thought acceptable) and two bracelets for her kindness.

The two bracelets for Rebekah's hands are of ten shekels weight in gold, ten being the sacred kabbalistic number corresponding to the Ten Commandments and intended to emphasize the spiritual level of the intended engagement. Once he has given Rebekah the gifts, Eliezer goes home with her to met her family, tells them who he is and all about his errand.

The next day, Eliezer asks if he can take Rebekah directly back to Canaan with him but her mother and brothers want to send her later, after ten days, so that they can say goodbye to her properly. (Other Hebrew translations suggest that it is ten months, not days, which was quite common – but it is still the noteworthy ten.) Eliezer is not happy with that so they send for Rebekah. It is noticeable that Rebekah is asked what her will might be in the matter. *"Then they called Rebekah and said to her, 'Will you go with this man?' And she said, 'I will go.'"* (Genesis 24:58.) The implication is that if she had said she would not go immediately, her opinion would have been honored. This is relevant because it shows a progression. Sarai/Sarah was not asked her permission when Abram/Abraham said she was his sister and the kings took her to their harem. It may seem like a minor example but each woman's story tells of a kernel of growth.

Rebekah and some handmaidens travel back with Eliezer and before they come to Abraham's tents they see Isaac in the fields. He comes towards them and Rebekah veils herself, as was considered modest (as Eliezer was only a servant she did not have to veil herself before him), and they introduce themselves to each other.

It says in the Bible that Isaac *"brought her into his mother Sarah's tent, and took Rebekah, and she became his wife; and he loved her: and Isaac was comforted after his mother's death"* (Genesis 24:67).

The marriage came before the love, not the other way around. According to Midrash and the *Zohar*, the purpose of marriage is service to God and not about love or lust. This may put a new complexion on Jesus' opinion that marriage was irrevocable: *"What therefore God hath joined together, let not man put asunder"*

(Mark 10:9). Nowadays very few marriages are made in the service of God so they are not what Jesus would call marriages at all. It also implies that God can put marriages asunder if they are no longer serving the couple or the higher purpose.

The *Zohar* says that on the death of Sarah, the blessings which had attended the household and the pious customs which distinguished it ended too. But when Rebekah was brought to the tent, they were restored. The Sabbath lamp once more illuminated the home of the Patriarchs and Rebekah continued all the other religious rites which Sarah had initiated.[38]

The *Zohar* goes further and talks about Rebekah's providing four different aspects of wifehood to Isaac. Taking Rebekah represents the physical World; marrying her, the psychological World; loving her, the spiritual World; and the reference to not missing his mother refers not so much to Sarah but to the Divine Mother.

For twenty years of her marriage, Rebekah is barren just like Sarah. But instead of just waiting for God to act in the matter, *"Isaac entreated the Lord for his wife, because she was barren: and the Lord was entreated of him, and Rebekah his wife conceived."* Here is evidence of a more equal relationship with God – as though Divinity is perceived more as a friend than a master. The *Zohar* says that Isaac's prayer meant that he rose above the planetary influences which had decreed Rebekah's infertility. Kabbalistic astrologers teach that free will can and will always overrule astrological influences which will only affect the lower aspects of our psyches. Contacting God directly is a powerful form of free will.

There is also evidence of a direct relationship between Rebekah and the Lord when Rebekah realizes that she has conceived twins and that they are fighting in the womb.

She went to enquire of the Lord. And the Lord said unto her, 'Two nations are in thy womb, and two manner of people shall be

separated from thy bowels; and the one people shall be stronger than the other people; and the elder shall serve the younger.'
Genesis 25:24

Isaac and Rebekah's sons Esau and Jacob are born. Midrash is curt to the point of cruelty on the difference between the brothers, saying that Jacob is born circumcised while Esau is born redheaded, implying that he would be violent. It claims that the name given him by his parents was an abbreviation: *Eisav – ha shav*, literally, 'this is worthless'.[39]

However, Isaac loves Esau and enjoys the meat that this rough hunter son brings for him. Rebekah loves Jacob and is angry with Esau because he marries two women from outside the family rather than keeping the bloodline pure. In the Torah, the terminology used in the Bible to describe Jacob is translated as his being a plain man, but the Hebrew *tam* can also mean 'perfect, complete'.

There's a telling scene where Jacob is cooking lentil stew and Esau comes back from hunting, starving. He asks Jacob for food and Jacob says he can have food in return for his birthright. Esau agrees without hesitation showing that he is a simple, animal man who didn't think of consequences. In fact, Esau cannot really sell his exoteric birthright because it is up to Isaac to decide which of his sons will be the one to inherit and it was always understood that Esau, the eldest and his father's favorite, will be given it automatically. But the birthright also meant the right to be the spiritual leader of the clan and the right to act as a priest and for this Jacob is suited where Esau is not. Also, the fact that Esau is willing to sell something so important to his younger brother in return for some food shows either that he is taking his spiritual birthright very much for granted – or that he doesn't really care. Neither of those attitudes will make him a strong man and a good leader, especially spiritually. Jacob knows this and decides to put it to the test.

In the meantime there is an interesting vignette. There is a famine in the land so Isaac and Rebekah head south. Genesis tells the story as well as anyone can.

> *And Isaac dwelt in Gerar: And the men of the place asked him of his wife; and he said, She is my sister: for he feared to say, She is my wife; lest the men of the place should kill him for Rebekah; because she was fair to look upon.*
>
> *And it came to pass, when he had been there a long time, that Abimelech king of the Philistines looked out at a window, and saw, and, behold, Isaac was sporting with Rebekah his wife.*
> Genesis 26:26–8

It doesn't say if it is the same Abimelech who took Sarah but, if so, he must have been suspicious from the start! What is very odd here is that sexual behavior in daylight was not permissible to the Hebrews (and it seems a rather odd thing to do in public if you are pretending to be brother and sister). The *Zohar* explains it by saying that Abimelech is an astrologer and that his study of the stars is the 'window' through which he can see the truth. So, he may have seen a chart which said that Isaac and Rebekah were lovers.

> *And Abimelech called Isaac, and said, Behold, of a surety she is thy wife: and how saidst thou, She is my sister? And Isaac said unto him, Because I said, Lest I die for her.*
>
> *And Abimelech said, What is this thou hast done unto us? One of the people might lightly have lien with thy wife, and thou shouldest have brought guiltiness upon us.*
> Genesis 26:8–10

So, this time, the story stops before the woman can be taken away. But even so, Isaac hasn't learnt any more than Abraham. We don't know what Rebekah thinks but, again, it is the foreigner, the one outside the tribe, who is demonstrating integrity.

When Isaac grows old he becomes blind (which could also refer to a psychological state) and wants to give his blessing to his eldest son Esau. Rebekah decides to take things into her own hands – to do God's will for him – and she tells her younger son to dress up as Esau and takes him to Isaac in his brother's place (Genesis 27:6–16). It was traditional for a father to give an official blessing to the son who was going to inherit his land and possessions before he died.

Isaac asks his elder son to go out and hunt some deer and to come back and cook it in the way that he likes most and then he will receive his father's blessing.

But Rebekah overhears what Isaac said and, remembering that God had told her that Jacob would be the one to rule Esau, she thinks that Jacob should receive the blessing. This is not only because she loves him more but also because Esau had married two women from local tribes who did not believe in the one God. Rebekah, as Isaac's widow, would no longer be in charge of the Sabbath lights or the rituals after his death – that was the responsibility of the wife of the man who held the birthright. Esau's wives probably did not even believe in the one God so they would not want to do the sacred ceremonies.

Rebekah tells Jacob to go and fetch a couple of young goats and says that she will cook them just the way that his father likes them and, because Isaac cannot see, he will bless Jacob instead of Esau and Jacob will receive God's Divine promise.

Now Jacob sees that this will not work, for his father will be able to hear, sense and feel the difference between the two men, but Rebekah has a plan. She cooks the kids in a savory sauce and puts their skins on Jacob's hands and neck so that he feels as hairy as Esau. When people lose their sight, their other senses become enhanced so she also gives Jacob some of Esau's unwashed clothes to wear so that Isaac will be able to identify his son by the scent of his clothing.

The trick works and Isaac blesses Jacob and makes him his spiritual heir. This blessing was regarded as irrevocable.

Commentaries say that Rebekah did the right thing to enable God's will but the attributes of the human soul, according to Kabbalah, are truth, discernment and mercy (the *Zohar* says these represent Yahweh directly). Rebekah is said to be God's instrument in what is a clear act of dishonesty and cheating. This is the level of ego and tribal consciousness, not soul. God does use people's strengths and weaknesses as part of the great plan but if people do things which are not honest, even for the best intentions, there will always be repercussions and Rebekah's actions have consequences that are savage and painful.

Esau threatens to kill Jacob and Isaac sends his younger son away, telling him to travel to Rebekah's relatives and find a wife from among the tribe. They may have thought that this exile was temporary but Jacob stays away for more than fourteen years and Rebekah loses her beloved son completely. As Isaac dies soon after, she is left alone, for Esau would not forgive her.

It's worth noting that Rebekah did not consult with God about the deception as she had over the twins in her womb; she was too eager to try and control the situation herself – just as Sarah did in giving Hagar to Abraham. This was a great loss of faith.

It's possible to surmise, from Esau's lifestyle, that he might have let Jacob have the heritage anyway or there might have been a Divine plan that Rebekah disallowed; one which would have brought her peace. But she was not willing or not able to trust that this would be the case.

Rebekah and the Tree of Life

Rebekah is placed at the sefira of *Yesod* which means Foundation. In modern interpretations of Kabbalah, this is the ego, our training and our reactions. Kabbalah teaches that our tribal, social and cultural beliefs are set in our minds by the age of seven.

These are full of 'shoulds' and rules. Some of these are excellent such as "look both ways when you cross the road." Some of them are ambiguous such as "do what I say, not what I do." But some of them are distinctly unhelpful such as, "*We* don't do that kind of thing" or "don't tell anybody what we did. It's our little secret."

Yesod is neither bad nor good; when it is balanced, it ensures that we can live comfortably within the family or tribe. If our family is dysfunctional, it lives within that paradigm, creating a co-dependent to an alcoholic mother, for example. It will adapt in whatever way will bring it the care and attention it needs. This is because Yesod is primarily a child. It is the child or servant of the sefira directly above it, Tiferet, which represents the true Self. The 'I' rather than the 'me'. A young child is not usually patient and prefers to reach out for what it wants rather than wait until the parent thinks it is appropriate for it to be given. A mother will tell a child not to eat cakes directly out of the oven because she knows both that they are too hot and that too many sweet things are bad for the little one. She also knows that the child must learn discipline.

But we humans are fallible and we generally learn best by experience. A burnt mouth or a sick stomach can teach us much more swiftly than an instruction which we may see as being contrary or unhelpful. And we learn according to what our parents do and are rather than what they tell us to do.

Midrash says of Rebekah:

Her father was a rogue and her brother was a rogue and the people of her town were likewise rogues, and this righteous woman who came forth from among them might well be compared to a lily among thorns.[40]

Blood will out and Rebekah, too, turns out to be a rogue.

Levels of Interpretation

Literally, Rebekah does what has to be done. She knows, as a mother, that Jacob will be the better leader of the family because he hasn't married unsuitable women from outside the tribe, he's not careless like Esau who is willing to give up his life's inheritance for a meal and she's sure he'll do a better job. The end justifies the means in her eyes.

She may also think she's doing God's will – the Rabbis in the Midrash certainly think that she is – and she *was* told that Jacob would be the leader. But, like Sarah, she's not capable of trusting God to be able to do it without her help. Rebekah knows full well that she is being willful no matter how the commentaries try to excuse her. Jacob says to her:

'My father peradventure will feel me, and I shall seem to him as a deceiver; and I shall bring a curse upon me, and not a blessing.' And his mother said unto him, 'Upon me be thy curse, my son: only obey my voice, and go fetch me them.'

She is willing to risk the negative consequences; Rebekah always had courage.

Obviously, God does use us as instruments of good but not usually when it comes to deception. The outcome of Rebekah's actions proves them to be the result of her own desire to control the situation, not from doing the Divine will. The story of Abimelech and how Isaac and she replicate Abraham and Sarah's deceit that they are not married shows that they are still not living in clear trust and that they expect others to hurt them when only good may be intended.

Allegorically it's a story about cause and effect which can only truly be understood when we come to Jacob's own story and his two wives, Leah and Rachel. It demonstrates that having strong willpower is both good and not-so-good. Rebekah knew her own will enough to be happy to go and live with total strangers at a moment's notice, but she was willful in creating the result she desired and it all blew up in her face.

Metaphysically, the story will either attract or repel us. Those who don't trust or relax into positive beliefs about what will happen, and feel they have to hurry the process along, will sympathize or approve of Rebekah's actions. They may be right! For others, however, it may be a signal to watch how they try to control the world. It's fine to have a guiding hand on the rein but not to act deceitfully to get the end we desire.

The mystical aspect shows that humanity *has* evolved just a little. Isaac intercedes directly for Rebekah's barrenness. Although the two of them deceive the foreign king, they act like husband and wife in public so they reveal the essential truths of themselves. But they are still very young souls on the pathway to consciousness.

Chapter Ten

Repeating Patterns – Leah and Rachel

Names: Leah. The name Leah originates from either the Hebrew *la ah* meaning 'weary' or 'to tire' or from *'le'ah'* meaning 'wild cow' or 'gazelle'. The latter does seem to be more likely, given the spelling and the fact that Rachel means 'ewe' although some translators say it also means 'one who is pure'.

Leah and Rachel's stories are so bound up in each other that they have to be told together. However, unlike Hagar, whose story is similarly tied to Sarah's, the two wives of Jacob are Matriarchs in their own right.

After being exiled from his family, Rebekah's son Jacob sought refuge with Laban, his maternal uncle, and asked to work for him. Laban asked what wages he required and Jacob, who had met Laban's younger daughter Rachel on the way and fallen in love with her, asked for her hand in marriage in return for seven years of work.

It was a lasting infatuation or genuine love for as Genesis says, *"Jacob served seven years for Rachel; and they seemed unto him a few days, for the love he had to her"* (Genesis 29:20). There is, however, no word of what Rachel felt for Jacob.

Rachel is always known as "Rachel the beautiful" but Laban's other daughter, Leah, is described as "tender-eyed". In the modern world we might see this as compassionate or loving; it might mean that she was blue-eyed (which would have been unusual) but it is more likely to have meant that she had weak eyes. Some somewhat far-fetched Rabbinical commentary says that Leah was originally destined to marry Esau, Jacob's elder brother, and her eyes were weakened by continual tears prompted by this prospect.

As the eldest daughter of Laban, Leah should have been the

one who married first – that was the correct order in those days and remained so in many cultures for thousands of years afterwards. Even in the UK, as recently as the early 20th century within the Middle and Upper Classes, it was deemed unfortunate for a second daughter to make her entrance into society if the first was not already betrothed.

On the day of Jacob's wedding to Rachel, Laban substitutes Leah for her sister, very neatly handing Jacob his Karma for his deceit of his father, Isaac. The substitution might not be as absurd as it seems, for the bride would have been very heavily veiled, but the fascinating point to the story is that Jacob doesn't appear to notice that he has been tricked until after the marriage is consummated which implies that Leah must have pretended to be Rachel and answered to her name at least.

And it came to pass, that in the morning, behold, it was Leah: and he said to Laban, What is this thou hast done unto me? did not I serve with thee for Rachel? wherefore then hast thou beguiled me?
Genesis 29:25

Laban replies that it is correct to marry the elder daughter first and strikes another deal with Jacob; that he can marry Rachel in seven days' time – after spending a week with Leah – if he agrees to serve another seven years for the younger daughter.

The Bible says nothing of Rachel's views – or even what happened to her when Leah took her place. Was she willing to have this deception carried out? Or was she hidden away against her will? And how did she feel about becoming the second wife to the socially superior first wife? However, the commentaries have plenty to say, telling us clearly that this was an agreement between Leah and Rachel made as a result of Rachel's kindness. Midrash says that Jacob and Rachel suspect that Laban may pull such a trick and devise a series of signs by which Jacob can identify the veiled bride on his wedding night. But when Rachel sees her sister being taken out to the wedding canopy, her heart goes out to her for the public shame Leah will suffer if she is exposed. Rachel therefore gives Leah the signs so that Jacob will not realize that there has been a switch.[41]

Laban's renegotiation is clever for, in that following week, Jacob gets Leah pregnant. From then on, the story becomes an incredible soap opera of jealousy and rivalry between Rachel and Leah. Even if Rachel did concede to her father's trick for Leah's sake, it must have been humiliating to experience such an outcome. It was no good being loved if you couldn't provide your husband with sons. Leah pops out four boys: Reuben, Simeon, Levi and Judah in quick succession with another two, Issachar and Zebulun, later on in the marriage. Jacob wanted sons and obviously appreciated Leah's fertility enough to continue sleeping with her even though Genesis makes it clear that he did not love Leah. *"And when the LORD saw that Leah was hated, he opened her womb: but Rachel was barren"* (Genesis 29:31).

It is clear that Rachel grieves for her infertility. She begs Jacob to help her but, unlike Isaac his father who entreated God on Rebekah's behalf, Jacob has no compassion for her.

> *Rachel envied her sister; and said unto Jacob, 'Give me children, or else I die.' And Jacob's anger was kindled against Rachel: and he said, 'Am I in God's stead, who hath withheld from thee the fruit of the womb?'*
> Genesis 30:1

Midrash adds an interesting rider: "Rachel envied Leah's good deeds. Rachel said: 'If Leah were not righteous, would she have given birth?'"[42]

Rachel, like Sarah before her, decides to offer her handmaiden to Jacob to have children on her behalf; Jacob accepts and Rachel raises Bilhah's two sons, Dan and Naphtali. There is no record of any hostility between birth and adopted mother but then Bilhah is not the mother of a single, longed-for child. Leah, who has at that time stopped bearing children, promptly retaliates with her own handmaiden, Zilpah, who gives birth to another two boys, Gad and Asher.

The bitter rivalry between the sisters does not end there. Midrash adds insult to injury, saying that as well as Jacob loving Rachel more than Leah, he even loves Bilhah, Rachel's handmaiden, more than he loves Zilpah, the handmaiden of Leah.[43]

One day Leah's eldest son, Reuben, finds some mandrakes which were said to have powerful fertility magic. Rachel asks for the mandrakes and Leah replies:

'Is it a small matter that thou hast taken my husband? And wouldest thou take away my son's mandrakes also?' And Rachel said, 'Therefore he shall lie with thee to night for thy son's mandrakes.'
Genesis 30:15

Jacob obliges and, as is the way with soap operas, Leah conceives again that night and gives birth to Issachar. Leah's fecundity obviously re-attracted Jacob as she then gives birth to Zebulun and to Dinah, the only girl child of the whole family.

Maybe it was the mandrakes ... but then *"God remembered"* Rachel and she bore her own first son, Joseph. What joy that must have brought to her. *"God hath taken away my reproach,"* she says (Genesis 30:22).

Jacob and his family end up leaving Laban's house and land and Rachel steals her father's *teraphim.* These were images of gods which would have been regarded as idols by followers of the Lord. The Rabbis justify the theft by saying that Rachel did it to save Laban's soul. *"She said: 'We are leaving – shall we leave this old man in his corruption?'"*[44] Another commentary says that Rachel stole these idols so that the gods of the images would not be able to tell Laban that they had left with his grandchildren and their flocks.[45]

What is far more likely is that these were fertility gods and that Rachel, like many of her contemporaries, having once conceived had put her faith in magical lore and household idols. Again, as with Rebekah's story, this is contradictory. Rachel had said that the Lord had been the one to help her give birth to Joseph so she knew that God could and would help her – but she was still hedging her bets as we all, so often, do.

Laban pursues the escapees and claims his idols back. Jacob does not know that Rachel had taken them, and tells him that whoever has stolen them will be put to death. But the teraphim are not discovered because Rachel puts them in her camel's saddle and sits on them. Midrash says that a miracle was performed for her and the idols were transformed into cups and therefore Laban cannot find them.[46] What is far more likely is that Rachel either was menstruating or said she was. The laws of cleanliness meant a man could not touch a seat where a menstruating woman had sat.

Rachel does conceive again but with fatal consequences. It is deeply ironic that she prophesied that she would die if she could not have children and then dies giving birth to Benjamin (Genesis 35:16–19).

Leah outlives her sister. She may never have been loved but she does become respected by her husband, and Jacob would ask her opinion as well as Rachel's before making decisions (Genesis 31:4 and 31:14). She was to live to observe the process of Karma in her own life, although this time it was enacted on her daughter rather than herself.

The Talmud and other Jewish commentaries bend over backwards to explain and excuse Leah and Rachel's behavior. They say that both women act as they do through a desire to grow spiritually through close contact with the *Zadik* – wise man or emissary of God – who is Jacob. By bearing his sons – all of whom become Zadikim in their own right and became the twelve tribes of Israel – they are developing their own close relationship with God.

Both women are said to have used the other's example in seeking such spiritual closeness as a means to expand her own.

But this was not spiritual behavior and cannot be excused as such. These are real women behaving badly – as so many real human beings do. Their position in the tribe was decided by how successful they were in producing male children and that was all that mattered. Leah and Rachel are revered simply as the mothers of the twelve tribes of Israel. We can learn a great deal from them but they are not an example of how to live a happy life or one of service to the greater good.

Leah and Rachel and the Tree of Life

Leah is placed at Hod on the left-hand column of the Tree. This is the feminine, passive or receptive side and Hod represents the sefira of the trickster, the thinker, the clever person who uses intelligence rather than intuition. Hod is also referred to as the sefira of reverberation; this is the physical manifestation of Karma.

Rachel is placed at Nezah, the sefira parallel to Hod on the right-hand column of the Tree. Nezah represents action, attraction, passion, thoughtlessness, instigation, eternity and physical beauty.

The pathway between Hod and Nezah is known as 'the liminal line'.[47] Below it we are acting unconsciously; above it we are capable of being aware of what we are doing. Leah and Rachel's stories boomerang backwards and forwards through action and reaction. The whole story hinges on Rachel's beauty and Leah's fertility. The two women appear to be two halves of a whole fighting each other with envy rather than working together.

Bilhah and Zilpah, the maidservants who are also given to

Jacob, are placed in two triads of the lower psyche (Hagar is in the third). There is little to choose between the two women but Bilhah's relationship with Rachel appears to be slightly more nurturing than Zilpah's with Leah. Rachel speaks lovingly of how Bilhah's child will also be hers. So I have placed Bilhah in the triad between Hod, Nezah and Yesod which is the triad of *willingness,* and represents the desire to be of service to the family or society. Bilhah, if she loved her mistress, would have been willing to help her, to alleviate her suffering. There is no quarrel between the women.

Zilpah is simply brought into play by Leah to match Rachel's gift of her maidservant. There is no need for another child for Leah, she has several; Zilpah is simply a weapon to be used against Rachel. Therefore, she is placed in the triad of Malkhut, Hod, Yesod, the triad of *will-lessness.* This is the place where no opinion is given, no action is taken; what is done to one is just taken for granted. It may be resented but no responsibility is taken and no action is initiated in order to resist or move away from it.

Levels of Interpretation

Literally, we see what happens when a marriage gets crowded. Although Rachel is the one Jacob loves, he is quite happy to continue to have sex with her fertile sister in order to have children. Rachel brought adultery into the marriage and into her own life by marrying a man who was already committed to another. Whether she had a choice is moot; the situation was set up from the moment that Jacob and Leah were married.

Allegorically we can see a pattern developing of jealousy between two women who are both striving to be first in the life of their husband. Like Sarah, Leah and Rachel are both willing and able to sacrifice the life of another for their own needs. Zilpah and Bilhah had no choice but to become Jacob's concubines and bear his children, whereas Leah and Rachel at least had some right to comply or object. They also had the choice to work together as partners rather than against each other. Had they done so, there would have been no adultery.

Metaphysically, we are invited to see where we, in our own lives, may have competed unfairly with another, stolen at any level or treated another human being as a thing rather than a person. This story is all tribal; we know nothing of how Leah or Rachel actually felt about Jacob; they are only concerned with their 'right' to have children. This maternal drive is a very powerful instinct which, for many women, cannot be denied. We believe that we all have the right to have a child. But do we? In the days of Genesis it was a commandment to have children but is that the same now in a world with such a huge population? It is worth considering where our own biological drives may rule our life to the detriment of our soul.

At the mystical level, we can see that the feminine within humanity has still learnt very little. It is still willing to manipulate others for its own gain and it still regards reproduction as its most vital role. It even seems to have taken a step back from the Divine. Neither Leah nor Rachel trust God or turn to prayer. The women's faith is in their own bodies or in magical techniques. In the end, Rachel's belief in household gods and mandrakes works but it does not bring her lasting happiness.

However, as we step out of the shoes of the Matriarchs, very real women who built the foundation that supports the feminine soul, we can move on to the explorers and heroines who made great leaps of faith both with and without the support of their tribe. These are the women of inspiration whose stories have so often been forgotten.

Part Four

Leaving the Tribe

Chapter Eleven

Dishonor and Shame – Dinah

From here on, we move above the liminal line between Hod and Nezah on the Tree of Life. Now, the Hebrew women began to attempt to leave the tribe behind and become individuals. Some succeed and some do not. Some, like Miriam, stay with the tribe itself but leave the land which they all inhabited to enter the wilderness together. Just because there is a new place to dwell does not mean that you leave the tribal consciousness behind.

This consciousness is the thought processes and the beliefs that we learn as children. We are taught what our society judges to be right and wrong (the Tree of Knowledge), what behavior is acceptable and what beliefs we should have. Some of us rebel but most conform in some way or another, even if it's only in the belief that rules and traditions are more important than happiness.

On the diagram of the Tree of Life, all the triads (triangles) and sefirot below Tiferet are subject to the beliefs of the tribe. The triad known as the 'Awakening Triad' between Hod, Tiferet and Nezah is where we begin to come into our own power and step away from learnt beliefs or habitual situations. However, as we step upwards and outwards, deep inner resistances come up as well as outer complaints and disagreement from others who wish us to remain as we used to be. I remember the wife of an old friend whose marriage was breaking up saying: "I want my old Paul back." He was attempting to leave that tribe and it could not be done without pain on both sides.

The triads on either side of Tiferet represent the instinctive movements or places of paralysis in our lives which will resist or promote our spiritual or personal growth, either driving us out of the tribe or pulling us back into it. The sefira of Tiferet is the first place on the Tree of Life where we can feel free and confident of our true relationship with God, the Universe and our fellow men.

Four women represent these complex psychological aspects of our own inner selves: Dinah, Miriam, Rahab and Ruth.

Dinah

Name: Dinah means 'judged' in Hebrew.

Dinah is Leah's daughter, the only girl child among twelve brothers and half-brothers. We know very little about her but we do know that a life she is given the opportunity to live (perhaps even happily) outside her family ties and tribal links is vetoed by her brothers.

Dinah is raped or seduced (the Bible doesn't make it entirely clear) by a man from a different tribe (Genesis 34:2–4). She goes out to visit *"the daughters of the land"* and Shechem, a prince in that country *"saw her and took her and lay with her and defiled her"* (Genesis 34:3). The word used for 'defiled' is *anah* and it is a translation that doesn't quite work. *Anah* means 'to humble'. That is relevant because in the *Book of Exodus* there's a phrase where the Israelites are told by God not to *anah* any widow or orphan – those of low social standing should not be humiliated nor lose what dignity and independence that they have. The general assumption is that Shechem rapes Dinah. It is also possible, however, that she consents but, in losing her virginity outside of marriage, she is 'defiled' according to the social mores of the times. Even today, in many parts of the world, a woman who loses her virginity outside marriage is seen as tarnished goods.

Shechem falls in love with Dinah. *"And his soul clave unto Dinah"* and his father, Hamor the Hivite, prince of the country through which Jacob and his family are travelling, goes to talk to Jacob about what had happened.

The sons of Jacob came out of the field when they heard it: and the men were grieved, and they were very wroth, because he had wrought folly in Israel in lying with Jacob's daughter; which thing ought not to be done. And Hamor communed with them, saying, 'The soul of my son Shechem longeth for your daughter: I pray you give her him to wife. And make ye marriages with us, and give your daughters unto us, and take our daughters unto you. And ye shall dwell with us: and the land shall be before you; dwell and trade ye therein, and get you possessions therein.'

And Shechem said unto her father and unto her brethren, 'Let me find grace in your eyes, and what ye shall say unto me I will give. Ask me never so much dowry and gift, and I will give according as ye shall say unto me: but give me the damsel to wife.'

Genesis 32:7-10

We do have to take our 21st century judgmental hats off here because the lore of the time was that Shechem could do whatever he wanted with any itinerant woman who was passing through his territory and who happened to be unwise enough to be out on her own. It was pretty unlikely that, after such an incident, a prince would take the woman home with him, offer her his hand in marriage and say that he and his father would take whatever terms her family set. He and his father even offer to merge tribes, and promote more interracial marriages. But Hamor and his subjects were not Hebrews, not followers of the one God, so this was deemed unacceptable.

We don't know what Jacob thinks but his sons take the matter into their own hands. It is clear that they have no intention whatsoever of letting Shechem marry Dinah but they pretend that they will agree on condition that every male in Hamor's city is circumcised: *"Then will we give our daughters unto you, and we will take your daughters to us, and we will dwell with you, and we will become one people"* (Genesis 34:16).

Shechem and all the males of the city are circumcised: they take to heart Hamor's decree that they will merge with the

Hebrews.

> *And it came to pass on the third day, when they were sore, that two of the sons of Jacob, Simeon and Levi, Dinah's brethren, took each man his sword, and came upon the city boldly, and slew all the males. And they slew Hamor and Shechem his son with the edge of the sword, and took Dinah out of Shechem's house, and went out... They took their sheep, and their oxen, and their asses, and that which was in the city, and that which was in the field, and all their wealth, and all their little ones, and their wives took they captive, and spoiled even all that was in the house.*

Genesis 34:25-29

Justified revenge or betrayal? That is up to you to decide. Whichever it is, we hear nothing more about Dinah. We don't know if she loved Shechem although we can surmise that her life as the wife of a prince might well have been more comfortable than the life of a woman judged to be impure and unmarriageable within her own tribe. At the end of the tale, when Jacob remonstrates with Simeon and Levi for what they have done, they reply, *"Should he deal with our sister as with a harlot?"* (Genesis 34:31). The word for whore or harlot is *zanah* and its use does imply that Dinah consented rather than was raped.

The commentaries vie with themselves to explain this story. Some say that it was a punishment for Jacob for delaying in his vow to God to set up an altar to the Lord at Bethel, others that it was retribution for living so long with Laban who was an idolater. Others say that it was Leah's punishment for trading with Rachel over the mandrakes. On the side of Dinah's innocence, the Talmud regards Shechem as a city of evil happenings: it is the place where his brothers sell Joseph into slavery and the place where the kingdom of the Davidic line are divided.[48] On the side of Dinah's guilt, Midrash claims that her action in going out represented a weakness from which all women suffer. As woman was created from the rib, a concealed place, she should not go out into public places.[49]

Dinah and the Tree of Life

Dinah's story fits into the left-pillar triad between Hod, Tiferet and Gevurah. This is the triad of passive emotion – pain, fear, self-denial, self-immolation and guilt. Dinah is silent throughout a tale of abuse and horror. This could be seen as making it a lesser story in our search for the Divine Feminine but it is significant that there is no voice at all. Sarah had contact with the Lord and frequently spoke with Abraham; Rebekah quizzed the Lord over the children in her womb; Rachel did not invoke the Lord but begged her husband to entreat Him for her to have a child. Leah only negotiated with Rachel for the mandrakes; she had no contact with the Lord herself and very little with her husband. Dinah is the daughter of Leah, the child of silence – but not a healthy silence. She 'went out' away from the tribe directly from Hod (her mother's placement on the Tree) and was unprotected; the implication here being that she had no contact with the Divine and no clear guidance from below either.

Climbing up the Tree represents human psychological and spiritual development and Kabbalah teaches that it is always best to hold the balance of both pillars equally to progress safely and securely. It is like paddling a boat: if you sit in the center, you can balance easily; but if you sit in the stern (Yesod) the boat will tip up so you cannot see where you are going; if you sit too far to the left or right, you will be out of balance and in danger of turning the boat over.

Dinah represents the soul who wishes to grow without the benefit of strong, helpful tribal beliefs and experience. In the modern world this is the person who gathers information from the Internet or from books and thinks they then know how to mend a car, run a seminar or run a marathon. Information is not knowledge. So Dinah went out without knowing the realities of the situation or, perhaps even worse, she was already nervous that she would be judged as having done something wrong. This triad expresses fear, guilt and revenge. In balance with the rest of the Tree of Life it can be equated with the conscience or caution; out of balance, it represents pain.

Dinah's brothers are the epitome of the out-of-balance aspect of this triad. They overreact by slaughtering hundreds for the crime of one who wished to make amends for his misdeed. In our psyches, we do this by hating and fearing those who have criticized or hurt us, or even more destructively, by hating ourselves for making mistakes or acting foolishly. Many a person has forbidden themselves ever to try again, whether it were to love, to get promotion or to grow, once they have made an error which hurt too much. If we don't strive to overcome our own self-reproach or guilt, we will live our lives in paralysis.

This triad can also represent the conscience. It touches the left-hand side of the Soul Triad of Gevurah, Tiferet and Hesed, and when we understand the emotions it brings up in us and examine them with clear thinking it will help us to understand when we are heading in a negative direction. However, doing this takes a level of awareness which requires a great deal of self-discipline.

Levels of Interpretation

At the literal level, Dinah's story is a reflection of the still-practiced tradition of honor-killing or vendetta. The tribe will not tolerate anyone who behaves outside of the accepted social or religious rules, punishing both their own and the other. Terrible deeds are justified in the name of protecting the tribal law and its people.

The inner story is complex. Firstly, it is about how often, when we try to step up or move on, we get slapped hard by circumstances or those we know. This usually happens when we are moving too fast for our own comfort or without consideration for others' feelings or for the basic rules of safety. There is an old proverb from Ghana: *"Softly, softly, catchee monkey."* Spiritual growth is rarely comfortable or convenient so it needs to be attempted with care and gentle persistence.

It also represents how we destroy our own opportunities or betray ourselves because we do not believe we are worthy of being, metaphorically, the bride of a prince. Or perhaps we have made one silly mistake or error of judgment, or done someone an ill turn, and our inner psyche punishes us by brooding on it and making the issue bigger and bigger. Or if someone has wronged us but apologized, we may not allow ourselves to believe that they have apologized in the *right* way and continue to throw blame at them for our situation. That often happens in a marriage break-up. Then whatever misfortunes may happen forever after can still be blamed on the ex.

At the mystical level we all, as part of humanity, have to choose to live globally together in order to achieve peace. The wider message is that we must link hands, link tribes and link cultures until there are no more divisions between us. It is wonderful to have diversity but to judge the other as being wrong or incomplete because they have different beliefs or patterns from us is the ever-open door to war.

At the metaphysical level, Dinah's story shows how all the Hebrew women's stories can be seen as the development of just one psyche – the slow realization of the Divine Feminine within us all. In that case, Dinah *is* her mother Leah and her experience is a direct reflection of Leah's theft of Jacob – whether or not it was unwitting – and her constant fear of being unloved and unworthy whatever she did. This kind of self-hatred draws negative experiences to it and can rarely teach its same-sex children not to make the same mistakes again.

Interestingly, the story continues with Jacob and his family leaving the area to travel to Bethel, and Jacob making them cleanse themselves of the idols which had become a part of their lives (whether physical or psychological). This indicates that the

Hebrews were *not* as focused on the one God as they presented themselves to be. They could, perhaps, have cleansed their own house rather than projecting their anger on to Shechem. This is still the case with the world today.

Chapter Twelve

Exodus from Egypt – Miriam

Name: The name Miriam is usually translated as 'bitterness'.

As there were no vowels in written Hebrew in Biblical times it would, most likely, have been written as MRM which leaves it open to interpretation. Most scholars believe that the first half of the word comes from the Hebrew *Marar* or *Mara*, meaning bitterness or strength. In the *Book of Ruth*, Naomi says, *"Call me not Naomi, call me Mara: for the Almighty hath dealt very bitterly with me"* (Ruth 1:20). However, some say it comes from *Meri*, meaning 'rebellious' or 'disobedient'. *Yam* is Hebrew for sea. Therefore *marar-yam* would mean bitter or strong sea. However, *Mayim* means water so it is possible that the name might be a construct of *Marar-mayim*, 'strong waters'.

The Marys in the New Testament were originally called *Maria* or *Mariam*.

The idea of bitterness fits because Miriam was born at the time when the Israelites' period of slavery in Egypt had reached its worst. However, I prefer the 'strong' interpretation, especially as Miriam was famed in legend for being the source of continual water for the Hebrews to drink in the wilderness. These were not bitter waters but nourishing ones.

The best-known story about Miriam is the narrative of Moses in the Bulrushes. The *Book of Exodus* tells how the Israelites were slaves in Egypt but were thriving in a way that threatened the Egyptians, so Pharaoh had decreed that all the male Hebrew babies should be killed.

At the beginning of the story, Moses' mother puts her newborn baby son in a cradle made of bulrushes and lets him float away down the river, trusting that he will reach safety. He does; the flowing water taking him to the feet of the one woman in all of Egypt who could possibly save him. Moses becomes the adopted son of Pharaoh's daughter who knows perfectly well that he is one of the Hebrews but who raises him as her own child. This is a wonderful story of two brave women who step away from the tribe. Jochebed trusts that God will save her son and is willing to give him up for a better future. The princess loves the child for himself, stepping above her father's decree.

Miriam follows the rush basket down the river and is brave enough to approach the all-powerful princess and to offer a wet nurse for the baby. The princess is quite aware that the woman proposed will be the child's mother and agrees to reunite them until Moses is weaned, when he becomes her adopted son.

Miriam's story is intertwined with flowing water from beginning to end. The Bible says nothing more of her until after Moses liberates the Hebrews from the rule of Egypt and they have crossed the Red Sea. Once the waters crash back on the pursuing horsemen, Miriam leads the celebrations.

And Miriam the prophetess, the sister of Aaron, took a timbrel in her hand; and all the women went out after her with timbrels and with dances. And Miriam answered them, Sing ye to the Lord, for he hath triumphed gloriously; the horse and his rider hath he thrown into the sea.
Exodus 15:20

The word for 'went out' is *yatza* and it is exactly the same word used for Dinah 'going out' in the previous story. But whereas for Dinah this was a bad thing, for the women who have left Egypt it is seen as a good thing. Possibly this is because it is a cry of triumph over an oppressing tribe rather than stepping away from the present one.

The next we hear of Miriam is a long time later following the giving of the Ten Commandments on Sinai after the Hebrews have spent many years wandering in the wilderness. Suddenly, she and her brother Aaron "spoke against" Moses because of the Cushite/Ethiopian woman whom he had married. It's not at all clear whether this refers to Zipporah, the wife Moses married before liberating the Israelites, or whether it is a second wife.

It is, however, fairly clear that matters are supposed to have moved on from the tribal view that marrying out of the tribe is a bad idea because the Lord turns up in a pillar of cloud and waxes exceedingly cross. When He has finished, Miriam has become leprous although nothing happens to Aaron.

Aaron asks Moses to intercede with God on Miriam's behalf and Moses does just that. God then says that the sickness will last just seven days. So Miriam becomes outcast for a week and the people wait for her recovery before they continue on their journey through the wilderness.

Together with her brothers, Moses and Aaron, Miriam is described in Midrash as part of a family triumvirate of leaders. This is a first – a woman as a leader. She doesn't have a title or a position but the Rabbis teach that she is just as vital to the story as Moses and Aaron. While Moses and Aaron are leaders for all the people, "Miriam is the teacher of the women."[50]

Midrash also claims a rather complicated reason behind the contradiction implied in Exodus 2:1 which introduces the story of Moses: *"And there went a man of the house of Levi, and took to wife a daughter of Levi. And the woman conceived, and bare a son."*

The issue here is that Jochebed and Amram already had two children, Aaron and Miriam, before Moses was born (as is related in Exodus 2:4 and in Exodus 7:7).

The Rabbis resolved this conundrum by explaining that Jochebed and Amram had divorced and Exodus 2:1 details their remarriage. They claim that when Amram realized that all the newborn boys were to be cast into the Nile, he divorced his wife because they would not be able to have more children. All the Israelite men apparently agreed and in consequence they also divorced their wives. Miriam, who was about five years old, is said to have persuaded her father to change his mind, saying:

"Father, Father, your decree is harsher than that of Pharaoh. Pharaoh only decreed against the males, but you have decreed against both the males and the females. Pharaoh decreed only for this world, but you decreed both for this world and the next. It is doubtful whether the decree of the wicked Pharaoh will be fulfilled, but you are righteous, and your decree will undoubtedly be fulfilled."
Pesikta Rabbati 43

She made Amram realize that he was preventing girls from being born at all and that any baby that was born and died as a result of Pharaoh's decree would still reach the World to Come; but an unborn child would never exist. Amram heeded his daughter, and remarried his wife.[51]

The Rabbis have a lot of fun with Miriam's condemnation of Moses' Egyptian wife, looking at her motivation for speaking out. They also examine why Miriam is punished but not Aaron.

Where it says in Numbers 12:1: "Miriam and Aaron spoke against Moses", they deduce that, because the word for 'spoke against' (*va-tedaber*) is a feminine singular form, Miriam spoke first and that is why she was punished and not her brother.

The topic of whether the Cushite woman was a second wife was a big problem, since the Torah does not state that Moses took another wife. So the Rabbis maintain that the Cushite woman was Zipporah and that the word 'Cushite' describes her fine qualities (her beauty and her actions) rather than her race. But if that is the case, there was no reason for Miriam and Aaron to find fault with her. The Rabbis then say that it's all about sex. Before the Revelation of the Torah to Moses, the Lord orders him to sanctify the people, bidding them: *"Be ready for the third day: do not go near a woman"* (Exodus 19:15).

After the Giving of the Torah, the Lord instructs Moses, *"Go say to them, Get you into your tents again. But as for thee, stand thou here by me"* (Deuteronomy 5:30–31), implying that Moses should still refrain from intercourse.[52]

There's a long debate about how Miriam could possibly have found out about this as Zipporah should have remained modest about her private life – which does rather show how little the Rabbis knew about gossip or women's confidences!

It is interesting, though, that Miriam is credited twice with speaking out over sexuality – to her brother and to her parents. In both instances she criticizes the one who withdrew from his wife. However, the Rabbis censure Miriam for not understanding that Moses' behavior was a special case because God was asking it of him.

Finally, there is the matter of Miriam's association with living water. In the Bible, Miriam's death is described in Numbers 20:1–2:

Then came the children of Israel, even the whole congregation, into the desert of Zin in the first month: and the people abode in Kadesh; and Miriam died there, and was buried there. And there was no water for the congregation: and they gathered themselves together against Moses and against Aaron.

The commentaries deduce from this that wherever Miriam went, there was water.

The people of Israel had three excellent leaders – Moses, Aaron and Miriam. Three good gifts were extended to the people of Israel on their behalf – the well, the clouds, and the manna. The well was provided due to the merit of Miriam, the clouds of glory because of Aaron, and the manna on account of Moses.[53]

After Miriam's death, Moses entreats the Lord for water and the Lord tells him to speak to a rock and it will give forth water (*mayim*). Instead, Moses strikes the rock with his staff. It duly produces a spring of water but the Lord chides him for not believing or obeying, and says that this disobedience means that he will not enter the Promised Land. The implication here is that Miriam *did* speak for water. Perhaps today we would call this affirmation or the power of prayer.

Miriam and the Tree of Life

Miriam represents the triad of Hod, Tiferet, Nezah – known as the 'Awakening Triad'. This is the place where people move on from the vegetable consciousness, which simply follows the tribe and the social mores of the day, and step up into animal consciousness. People at this level are known in Kabbalah as 'Uncommon People'. In the *Zohar*, Aaron is placed at the sefira of Hod, and Moses at Nezah so Miriam is held safely in the center between them as they support her development, as represented by the Exodus from slavery (Egypt) into the wilderness of spiritual growth. She stands in the center with one hand holding the right-hand column of the Tree of Life and the other holding the left-hand column. This is in stark contrast to Dinah who has no support at all and falls by the wayside.

Animal people can be very ambitious and proud, but they are those who will lead the way rather than follow existing trends. This stage of development can be a difficult one as family and friends often don't like it when we step up and move away from the norm. Miriam and her brothers were the leaders and the Israelites the 'vegetable people'. Once the excitement had died down after they had left Egypt and crossed the Red Sea, the people reacted against their leaders as the lower psyche often will.

And the people spake against God, and against Moses, "Wherefore have ye brought us up out of Egypt to die in the wilderness?"
Numbers 21:5

We see this every day in people reacting against governments and other powerful people and institutions. It is far easier to criticize the leaders than it is to step up and lead ourselves.

It is also hard to maintain spiritual growth – as Miriam shows by reverting to the social lore of her people by criticizing Moses for marrying outside the tribe. Retribution for that is swift and anyone who is working on their own development will recognize that, on the mystical path, any footfall to either side is more painful than any mistake made before the awakening to Spirit. In Miriam's case, she metaphorically lets go of the right-hand pillar and loses her balance, hitting the pain triad of retribution. It is perhaps because of her usual balance that she is the one punished. Aaron is only linked to one side of the Tree of Life so would not be expected to be as aware as his sister. It is usually the ringleader or the one who should know better who is punished by a teacher or parent.

Levels of Interpretation

There is no historical evidence of the Exodus from Egypt although it has provided inspiration to the Jewish nation for millennia through the festival of Passover. It is, however, one of the great stories of all time – the leaving of home to go on a dangerous expedition. Joseph Campbell calls it the Hero's Journey and it is something that every spiritual seeker must do at some time.

The most important part of Miriam's story is her connection with the water of life. Living water is always associated with ritual cleansing. Fresh, flowing water, not water from a still source, was required for any ritual bath (*mikvah*). And there is plenty of evidence in the Bible to support the association of living water with the Temple.

"*And Isaac's servants dug in the valley, and found there a well of springing [living] water*" (Genesis 26:20). In his commentary on the Torah, Rabbi Moses ben Nachman (Nachmanides) wrote: "'*A well of living waters' alludes to the House of G-d which the children of Isaac will build."*

The Roman historian Tacitus also gave a reference that the Temple at Jerusalem had, within its precincts, a natural spring of water that issued from its interior.[54]

Spring water is also mentioned in numerous ways throughout the Psalms as the "waters of salvation" that come from the Throne or House of God. Spring waters were an essential part of Temple requirements and must accompany any future Temple.[55]

Even more tellingly, there is the blood and water which sprang from the side of Jesus when he was pierced with the Roman soldier's spear (John 19:34). Jesus is believed to have been the personification of the essence of the holy of holies within the Temple and he teaches that those of faith will become the same as he. He speaks of living water to the Samaritan woman in John 4:10 and says: *"He who believes in me, as the Scripture has said, from out of his belly will flow rivers of living water."* The Greek word *koilia* translated as 'belly' can also mean the innermost part of a human or the womb. The word *hudor* for 'water' frequently means the water of a river or a fountain.

So the living water is Divinity. Miriam drew the living water to her wherever she went. She is the personification of the Divine Feminine entering exile with her people on the long road from slavery, through the wilderness of growth and experience, to the Promised Land of spirit.

Chapter Thirteen

Changing Tribe – Rahab

Name: Rahab means 'wide' or 'spacious' in Hebrew.

The story of Rahab takes place in the *Book of Joshua* once the Israelites have reached the Promised Land.

Instead of it all being milk and honey, as they believed that it would be, they have to fight for their right to be in this new country. That is often the case when we have a great goal we want to achieve but we don't truly believe that we deserve it, and we find ourselves experiencing all sorts of obstacles in the way.

Most of us have heard the story of the trumpets that brought down the walls of the city of Jericho. But before that comes Rahab's part in the affair. Unlike Mary Magdalene, who was unjustly inflicted with harlotry by Pope Gregory the Great five hundred years after the event, Rahab actually is a prostitute. She lives in Jericho.

Joshua is the leader of the Israelites after Moses' death and he sends spies to Jericho to see how the land lies. They get into the city and lodge at Rahab's house (we don't hear in what way). But, as so often happens, spies discover the spies and the king of Jericho sends soldiers to Rahab ordering her to give up her guests.

She tells them that there had been two men but they have already left and, if the king's men set out fast, they may just catch them outside the city.

The Hebrew spies she successfully hides in piles of flax on the roof of her house. Then, she tells them that she knows that the Lord (Yahweh) has given the land to the Israelites; the stories of the crossing of the Red Sea and the defeat of two kings of the Amorites, who had tried to block the Hebrews from living in the Promised Land, had reached Jericho and caused great consternation.

> *And as soon as we had heard these things, our hearts did melt, neither did there remain any more courage in any man, because of you: for the Lord your God is in heaven above, and in earth beneath. Now therefore, I pray you, swear unto me by the Lord, since I have shown you kindness, that ye will also show kindness unto my father's house, and give me a true token. And that ye will save alive my father, and my mother, and my brethren, and my sisters, and all that they have, and deliver our lives from death.*
> Joshua 2:9–13

The men agree; she lets them down by a cord through the window (her house was part of the town wall) and they charge her to tie a scarlet cord to the same window so that, when Jericho is taken, the Israelites will know where she lives and spare her family, on condition that they remain within the house.

The Israelites take the city, lay waste to everything and set fire to it. But Joshua tells the two spies to fetch Rahab and her family and keep them safe *"and she dwelleth in Israel unto this day; because she hid the messengers, which Joshua sent to spy out Jericho"* (Joshua 6:25).

Rahab and the Tree of Life

Rahab is placed in the triad of pleasure and addiction on the right-hand column of the Tree of Life. As we are climbing the Tree in the process of spiritual growth, she represents moving from the place of shame and degradation to the place of safety – the exact opposite of Dinah.

This triad is all about seeking what feels good for you; it can be a triad of great blessing or, in the case of addiction, of rebounding pleasure and pain. It is a place of mercy which can be over-merciful and overactive and, when experienced negatively, will mean that lessons are not learnt. You could place the serial monogamist here – the person moving on from one liaison to another without pausing to consider why each relationship fails or how much others might be hurt.

Rahab has already stepped outside the accepted mores of tribal consciousness before she meets the Hebrew spies. Joshua 2:15 says: *"for her dwelling was at the outer side of the city wall and she lived in the actual wall"* – the implication being that she acts as a prostitute for the people both inside and outside the city (tribe).

Her beauty and her immorality are her positive and negative links with Nezah (Rachel was also beautiful and she stole the teraphim from her father); she is merciful to the spies and although she betrays her tribe she does so through a belief that the Israelites' God is the true God. How you feel about her action is up to you. It is certainly selfish but, as she believes in the power of the Hebrews and their God and the alternative to not helping them would be death, it is her only way to save her family.

Levels of Interpretation

Literally, Rahab commits a huge act of betrayal of her people while defending her own life and the lives of her family. However, there is no implication that she continues with her life as a harlot. In fact, the Talmud teaches that Rahab marries Joshua following her conversion to the Israelites' faith.[56] As her reward, her daughters marry *kohanim*, members of the priestly caste, and their sons serve at the altar of the First Temple.[57]

Betrayal takes place at many levels. Even the great betrayal of Christ by Judas is open to several different levels of interpretation apart from the traditional Christian one that he was an evil man.[58]

Allegorically, Rahab's betrayal of her tribe, to the extent that it is annihilated, refers to killing off the lower aspects of the psyche which oppose spiritual growth; this is all about the spiritual seeker's learning to believe that he or she deserves the Promised

Land, the people of Jericho representing the parts that do not believe. It appears to be very similar to the story of Dinah where Shechem and his people are slaughtered by Jacob's sons but the two stories are diametrically opposed. In Dinah's story the possible development and expansion of the tribe is killed by the lower ego; in Rahab's the higher level – the soul – is the winner with the opposing resistance destroyed.

At the metaphysical level, we have to come to realize that moving on and up is always going to affect those around us and it may very well appear to be an act of cruelty. It may take a saint to leave behind a life of affluence where one is to take over the family business (such as St. Francis did) and it may mean that the business falls apart but, when God calls, we must go or our souls will shrivel and die. If our leaving causes destruction then it is worth considering whether too much weight is standing on our shoulders. When we leave for God's work, those behind may learn to stand on their own two feet.

However, if we find that each new situation becomes the same as the one before and choose repeatedly to move on, leaving ever more people behind us, then we are in the negative aspect of this level. It is important to learn from experience, and to understand that situations that repeat in our life cannot be erased by continually running away. They must be dealt with consciously.

That there is a place for the Divine Feminine in Rahab's story is indicated when, after the danger to the spies she had hidden had passed, Rahab advises them to: *"Make for the hills, so that the pursuers may not come upon you. Stay there in hiding three days"* (Joshua 2:16). Three days is always a significant time, representing the Trinity of I Am, Yahweh and Elohim or the Trinity of Father, Son and Holy Spirit. Midrash adds that the Divine Presence rests upon Rahab until the Israelites enter Jericho, for she knows that they will return after three days.[59]

Because Rahab is not frightened of the Israelites when they come to win Jericho, the Rabbis applied to her Proverbs 31:21:

"She is not afraid for her household because of snow, for her whole household is dressed in crimson" – the crimson being said to represent the *"length of crimson cord"* that would be the sign between them.[60]

This is one of the reasons behind the Middle Eastern practice of tying a red cord around the wrist for protection from the evil eye. In modern day Kabbalah, however, it most frequently refers to a red cord tied around Rachel's tomb. This is still viewed as a token of protection even though Rachel's own life was not one of happiness or safety.

Chapter Fourteen

Awakening to Change – Ruth

Name: Ruth means 'friend' or 'companion'.

The *Book of Ruth* is one of only two books in the Bible which are named for a woman. As we step out of the lower half of the Tree of Life and into the realm of the true Self beyond the ego, we begin to find the women who are independent, powerful and who change the course of history. From now on, we are dealing with women of destiny.

The Books of Ruth and Esther are especially significant because they both involve women who marry outside their tribe. The men are important to the story – and both are commanding leaders – but it is the decisions of the women which allow the stories to become so powerful. Like the Elohim, the women metaphorically say, "let there be light." They create the space where the miracles can happen.

Ruth's story takes place in the time of the Judges. These were tribal rulers or military leaders who ruled the Hebrew people after Joshua and the Israelites had conquered Canaan, but before the establishment of the first Kingdom of Israel. The Judges were believed to be sent by God to deliver the people from a threat in wartime and to administer justice in peacetime.

The most striking aspect of Ruth's story is that she is not a Hebrew, she is a Moabite. But she marries an Israelite, the son of Elimelech and Naomi who have moved to her country because of a famine in their hometown of Bethlehem in Judah.

Elimelech dies in Moab, and Naomi's sons Mahlon and Chilion marry sisters Ruth and Orpah. This great sin of marrying out is explained in Midrash by the proposition that both Ruth and Orpah were daughters of the King of Moab, and therefore royal princesses.[61] Why that excuses it is not clear. The marriages lasted for ten years, although there is no mention of any children, and it is accepted by the commentaries that neither Ruth nor Orpah converted to Judaism at that time.

Then both Mahlon and Chilion die, and Naomi decides to return to Bethlehem. The famine is over and she can feel her homeland calling. To start with, both Ruth and Orpah travel with her but she speaks to dissuade them, saying they can marry again in Moab but that she has no more sons to offer them. Orpah turns back but Ruth insists on continuing with Naomi, saying some of the most beautiful words in the Hebrew Testament:

Entreat me not to leave thee, or to return from following after thee: for whither thou goest, I will go; and where thou lodgest, I will lodge: thy people shall be my people, and thy God my God.
Ruth 1:16

Midrash expands this into a discussion between the two women and declares it to be the process of conversion by Ruth to Judaism. Their very first walking together is understood as a discussion of the laws of conversion.[62] It's extremely important that Ruth is seen to have converted fully as she is the great-grandmother of King David and doubt has been placed on the Davidic line because of her origins.

One Midrash claims that Naomi is ashamed of Ruth and suspicious of her, but generally the commentaries bend over backwards to make her a fit ancestor for Israel's kingly line.

The two women arrive back in Bethlehem at the time of the barley harvest. They obviously have no money because Ruth offers to go gleaning. This was the practice of gathering up any corn which was not gathered into sheaves during the official harvesting. Whatever was left could be collected and taken away by the poor who had no land of their own. Gleaning was always allowed by any landowner as it was part of the Mosaic law:

And when ye reap the harvest of your land, thou shalt not wholly reap the corners of thy field, neither shalt thou gather the gleanings of thy harvest. And thou shalt not glean thy vineyard, neither shalt thou gather every grape of thy vineyard; thou shalt leave them for the poor and stranger.
Leviticus 19:9–10

Ruth goes to glean in the fields belonging to a kinsman of Elimelech. The owner of the land, Boaz, notices her. If you read between the lines you might think that he found her attractive; he certainly approved of her but he spoke to Ruth with the word *bath* which means 'daughter' so, to start with at least, his intentions are purely paternal.

Midrash says that Boaz is twice as old as Ruth and recently widowed. In the Hebrew Testament he instructs her to follow his own female servants and tells her that he has told his men not to lay a finger on her. When Ruth asks why he is being so kind, Boaz answers:

It hath fully been shewed me, all that thou hast done unto thy mother in law since the death of thine husband: and how thou hast left thy father and thy mother, and the land of thy nativity, and art come unto a people which thou knewest not heretofore. The Lord recompense thy work, and a full reward be given thee of the Lord God of Israel, under whose wings thou art come to trust.
Ruth 2:11–12

He invites Ruth to eat with the harvesters at lunchtime and, when she goes out to glean again, he instructs his men to leave handfuls of grain behind specifically for her. Ruth gleans for several weeks throughout the barley and wheat harvests, and is able to take a great deal of grain home; more than enough to take care of Naomi and herself.

However, girls will be girls ... and Naomi develops a cunning plan. She realizes that Boaz's attentions to Ruth are fairly marked and instructs her daughter-in-law to test them out. This is a fairly dramatic directive because, had they been misinterpreted, they would have marked Ruth down as a harlot. Naomi instructs her to go back to where Boaz and his people are celebrating the feast at the end of the harvest, to wait until they have eaten and drunk and then, when they sleep, in the same barn as they had eaten, to go and lie down next to Boaz and "uncover his feet". Ruth does just that.

> *And it came to pass at midnight, that the man was afraid, and turned himself: and, behold, a woman lay at his feet. And he said, 'Who art thou?' And she answered, 'I am Ruth thine handmaid: spread therefore thy skirt over thine handmaid; for thou art a near kinsman.' And he said, 'Blessed be thou of the Lord, my daughter: for thou hast shewed more kindness in the latter end than at the beginning, inasmuch as thou followedst not young men, whether poor or rich. And now, my daughter, fear not; I will do to thee all that thou requirest: for all the city of my people doth know that thou art a virtuous woman.'*
> Ruth 3:7–11

This is an interesting story for the Rabbis of the Midrash to get their heads around. To do so, they are at pains to emphasize Ruth's modesty while she was gleaning. She kept her skirts down so nothing of her legs could be seen, turned her face away so no man could see it and didn't even let one of her fingers show.[63] All the more incredible that she went to lie down with Boaz in the nighttime.

There's a common rumor around Biblical circles that the Hebrew word translated as 'feet' (*marjelah*) also means 'penis'. This is certainly not mentioned in the commentaries, but the implication is that Ruth demonstrated a willingness to have sex with Boaz. It is just possible; the word most often used in the

Hebrew Testament for feet is *regal*. Where *marjelah* is used elsewhere, in the *Book of Daniel*, it is translated variously as 'feet' or 'legs' and it is said to mean 'anything below the waist'.

However, Boaz, who wakes in surprise ('shock' is a slightly better translation than the KJV's 'afraid'), still refers to Ruth as "my daughter", and praises her virtue. In saying he will do *"all that thou requires"*, Boaz is not implying that Ruth is asking him to make love to her; he is referring to a law based on a teaching from Genesis 38:8: *"Go in unto thy brother's wife, and marry her, and raise up seed to thy brother."* The word 'wife' refers to a widow. So Boaz knew that Ruth was asking him to honor that teaching and either to marry her or to find a closer kinsman who would do so. He reassures her that everyone knows that she is an honorable woman and that he will do just that. In the morning, he ensures that no one sees her and gives her six measures of barley to take back to Naomi.

Boaz is praised highly for his restraint and his words. One of the Rabbis says that Ruth was so very beautiful that whoever even saw her "would have an emission".[64] However, Boaz places his faith in the Lord and is as well-behaved as any ancestor of the kingly line should be.

Naomi's advice to Ruth, once her daughter-in-law has told her what happened is, *"Sit still, my daughter, until thou know how the matter will fall: for the man will not be in rest, until he have finished the thing this day"* (Ruth 3:18). Ruth has done her part; now she must wait for Boaz to do his.

Boaz goes to the city gate, where people meet up, and finds the kinsman who is closer to Naomi's family than he and then he gathers ten elders of the city – ten was the required *quorum* for any sacred service or decision to be considered valid. He asks the kinsman if he is willing to buy land that Naomi had to sell on behalf of her late husband. The man agrees. Then Boaz says, *"What day thou buyest the field of the hand of Naomi, thou must buy it also of Ruth the Moabitess, the wife of the dead, to raise up the name of the dead upon his inheritance"* (Ruth 4:5). The kinsman declines – and by some commentaries this is seen as evidence that Ruth had not converted and the kinsman is honoring the Mosaic law that a Jew may not marry a Moabite: *"An Ammonite or Moabite shall not enter into the congregation of the Lord; even to their tenth generation shall they not enter into the congregation of the Lord for ever"* (Deuteronomy 23:3).

Some retrospective amending of the law was required in the commentaries to get around this problem and the result was that the ban was declared to be limited to males and not females, given that the words are not Moabitess or Ammonitess.[65]

Boaz declares before the quorum that he will buy the land and take Ruth as his wife. The men bless the transaction and Boaz and Ruth are married and take Naomi into their home. They have a son, Obed, who becomes the ancestor of King David. However, in a final attempt to add gravitas and sanctity to the story, the Rabbis decreed that Boaz dies on his wedding night so that neither he nor Ruth obtain any "personal benefit" from the relationship: it is purely to give Naomi a grandson and ensure the Davidic line.[66]

Ruth and the Tree of Life

Ruth is placed at Tiferet, the *sefira* of the true Self where beauty and truth are perfectly balanced, and where the three Worlds of Asiyyah, Yezirah and Beriah meet. A person in Tiferet is directed by spirit, centered in their psyche and in perfect control of their physical body. Tiferet is often seen as the place of the heart, and it is the gateway to the human soul. The negative aspect of Tiferet is pride.

Ruth admires Naomi and her beliefs and follows her heart, stepping away from her own tribe and all that is familiar. She chooses Naomi's belief for herself and is willing to risk poverty and the humiliation of being seen as an unworthy foreigner for the sake of her soul. If she truly were the daughter of the King of

Moab, this is an exceptional decision. Ruth has to walk away from any pride in her lineage and the comfortable life that she might have had.

Courage is one of the attributes of Tiferet and, in obeying Naomi and approaching Boaz in the night, Ruth risks every ounce of her reputation. But she trusts that both Naomi and Boaz have seen her true worth and that she will be safe.

After that night she waits, again on Naomi's instruction. The ego would have pushed to get the decision sorted. The implication is that Ruth stands back and allows the results to unfold knowing that all is in Divine order. She does her part and lets it be.

Tiferet is the gateway between spirit and tribal consciousness; the place where we can become the watcher of our own motives and actions. We can bring spirit to the lower psyche, and new thought and new ways to enhance and transform former actions and beliefs. In Ruth's case this works down into the physical World with new blood to strengthen the Judaic line.

Levels of Interpretation

According to Deuteronomy, Ruth's story is impossible; she should not have been able to marry into Judaism once, let alone twice. However, laws are generally only made when the crimes for which they are created have already happened. And, of course, if Deuteronomy were an added aspect to the Hebrew Testament after the fall of the First Temple, the story might not be as unlikely.

As an allegory, it tells us that nothing is impossible if we are prepared to follow our heart although, to start with, we may be faced both with poverty and challenges to our pride. However, should we persevere and stay true to ourselves, we will find true prosperity at all levels.

The timbre which flows through this story at the metaphysical level is that Ruth is, in heart and soul, a Hebrew who has for some reason been born in exile. Everything conforms for her to return to her true place. She is Shekhinah for, despite her incredible beauty, no one could possibly mistake her for anything other than a modest, even perfect, woman. Her story has parallels to that of Rahab but the progression is that Ruth is virtuous from the very beginning. She is given the chance to become immodest but even when doing that which, in most women, would be seen to be the action of a harlot, she is still perceived to be totally honorable.

Here, the Divine Feminine is returning in beauty, strength and virtue. She has become the mother of the King again.

Part Five

Being the Vessel

Chapter Fifteen

The Dark Side – Deborah and Jael

Names: Deborah, *Dvora*, in Hebrew, means 'bee'.

Jael, *Ya'el* in Hebrew, is the name of the Nubian Ibex, a kind of mountain goat. As 'El' is one of the names of God, and *ya'* is Hebrew for 'shovel' and *ya'ah* means 'to brush aside' it could – at a stretch – have a more unique meaning as will be seen by the story.

Deborah was the fourth Judge of Israel, before the monarchy began with King Saul and continued with King David. Her story is intertwined with Jael's and it works at the soul level of the Tree of Life. At this level it is the women themselves who matter; the *Book of Judges* says that both are married but their decisions and actions have nothing to do with their husbands.

The narrative begins by telling us that Israel *"again did evil in the sight of the Lord"* (Judges 4:1), implying that the Hebrews began to worship idols. Because of this, the Lord had given them over to their enemies. In the time of Deborah, they were being ruled by Jabin, king of Canaan, whose chief officer was Sisera, the commander of nine hundred chariots. This fearsome force had oppressed the Israelites for twenty years.

> *And Deborah, a prophetess, the wife of Lapidoth, she judged Israel at that time. And she dwelt under the palm tree of Deborah between Ramah and Bethel in mount Ephraim: and the children of Israel came up to her for judgment.*
> Judges 4:4–5

This was phenomenal for the time – that a woman was leader of the tribe of Israelites and revered as a lawgiver and prophet in her own right. Midrash has quite a problem with it, bending over backwards to accuse Deborah of pride and bringing her back into second place behind the men. But the Hebrew Testament is clear: Deborah is king in all but name.

The Israelites cry out to the Lord for help and Deborah sends for the Israelite army leader, Barak, telling him that the Lord has promised him a victory if he will follow her instruction. He, in turn, says that he will only go and fight if Deborah comes with him. *"And she said, I will surely go with thee: notwithstanding the journey that thou takest shall not be for thine honor; for the Lord shall sell Sisera into the hand of a woman"* (Judges 4:9).

This is a strange prophecy – women did not fight in those days.

The two military commanders go to the appointed place and the two tribes engage in battle. The Israelites win and all those who have not been killed commit suicide – apart from Sisera who escapes.

He flees onto neutral ground, to the tent of Jael, wife of Heber the Kenite. Jael goes out to meet him, invites him in, assures him he will be safe and covers him with a rug. He asks her for water; she gives him milk. He asks her to watch at the door of the tent while he sleeps and to say that there was no one there if anyone asks.

> *Then Jael, Heber's wife, took a nail of the tent, and took an hammer in her hand, and went softly unto him, and smote the nail into his temples, and fastened it into the ground: for he was fast asleep and weary. So he died.*
> Judges 4:21

When Barak comes in hot pursuit, Jael goes out to meet him and shows him Sisera's body.

> *So God subdued on that day Jabin the king of Canaan before the children of Israel.*
> Judges 4:23

As might be expected there is plenty of commentary about Jael's action. In the wider world, it is seen as a breach of the fundamental laws of hospitality. Exodus 23:9, Leviticus 19:33 and several other texts expressly forbid the oppression or deceit of a guest. A somewhat strange and frightening example of this is the story of Lot who was willing to let townsmen of Sodom rape his virgin daughters rather than let the men harass two strangers (said to be angels) who were visiting him. This is a story to show the evil ways of the men of Sodom, which was destroyed immediately afterwards.

Several *Midrashim* add a sexual component to Jael's story, saying that Sisera had intercourse with her up to seven times. She is absolved from blame in this – on the assumption that either it is rape or that she engages in sex in order to exhaust him so that she can kill him.[67] In this she is praised above the Matriarchs who had sex for pleasure and for the procreation of children, and who were jealous of other women.

Yet another Midrash equates Jael with the Woman of Worth from Proverbs: *"She sets her hand to the distaff"* because she does not kill Sisera with a conventional weapon but with a tent peg and with the strength of her hands.[68] A distaff is a stick on which wool is held before it is spun on a spinning wheel.

Deborah returns to the story after the death of Sisera with what is known as "the Song of Deborah" where she tells Jael's story again in a paean of praise similar to one of the psalms. It includes the lines: *"Blessed above women shall Jael the wife of Heber the Kenite be, blessed shall she be above women in the tent"* (Judges 5:24).

Midrash explains that Deborah used her song to educate Israel to walk in the ways of the Lord, to study and to pray: it is one of ten songs of praise from the Hebrew Testament which form the foundation of the poetry of the Jewish people.[69] However, Deborah is also accused of pride and the power of prophecy is said to have been taken away from her in punishment.[70] This commentary also blames Barak for ceding power to her and says that to him should have been the victory and the song. The Rabbis are clearly uncomfortable with the idea of a powerful warrior-woman and are desperate to restore the male supremacy that was the norm at the time. They also are at pains to point out the importance of her relationship with her husband, Lapidoth, although they ascribe great worth to her in her assistance to him to be a good man.

In the first of her book series on *The Mother of the Lord*, Dr. Margaret Barker ascribes a different meaning to Deborah's marriage, saying that the Hebrew in Judges 4:4 is more likely to be translated as 'lady of the lightnings/flames/torches' than 'wife of Lapidoth', the latter being an otherwise unknown name and the Hebrew word *lpyd* meaning torch, flame or lightning. Dr. Barker also points out that Deborah sits under a palm tree, this tree being one of the main decorations of Solomon's Temple (1 Kings 6:29). An altar to the cult of Asherah, also decorated with palm trees, was found at Ta'anach, the site of the Israelite battle (Judges 5:19) linking Deborah directly with Asherah.[71]

Deborah, Jael and the Tree of Life

Both Deborah and Jael are placed at the sefira of *Gevurah* which means severity, strength, judgment, discernment and decision-making. Deborah is the passive strategic aspect of Gevurah and Jael is the active, martial aspect.

Gevurah is generally the most unpopular of the *sefirot* for the student in Kabbalah because it represents the place of commitment. For the person attempting to grow, the path to individuation at Tiferet can be exciting or, at least, interesting as they learn about the aspects of their own psyche from ego to Self. But once they have passed that level of 'enlightened self-interest' they must face the self-discipline of true spiritual growth, whether that means study, meditation, prayer or some other act of commitment.

Gevurah is placed on the left-hand feminine column of the Tree of Life, and it is best married with its parallel sefira of *Hesed* or Mercy on the right-hand column. However, there are times in our lives when we have to make clear decisions, cut out the dead wood and act to change a situation. Where Hesed is 'yes', Gevurah is a clear and resounding 'no'.

Many people become confused at how such a warlike sefira is placed on the passive column but Gevurah is associated with martial arts. These use the strength and the speed of the opponent to overcome the enemy. Strategy and placement are essential but just one blow at the right moment of the other's weakness is far more powerful than engaging in a sustained fight. Gevurah is also associated with the warrior as the defensive, rather than the offensive, role. The true soldier has the self-discipline to see his duty clearly, the discernment to recognize a real threat, rather than just posturing, and the judgment as to when and how to strike in order to remove or contain that threat.

Jael's placing here is clear to see: she waits until Sisera is asleep and with one blow removes the whole problem.

The Rabbis in Midrash call Jael a convert to Judaism. However, there is no indication of this in the *Book of Judges*; Jael is neutral and there is her strength. She has no anger for Sisera; she has no side to take; she simply wishes to end a war which has most likely laid waste to the land for twenty years. She is like a Samurai dispensing justice; she would most likely have done the same had the victory not gone to the Israelites and Barak had come to her for shelter.

The Kenites were a nomadic people who were metalworkers and smiths. According to Judges 1:16, Moses' father-in-law, Jethro, was a Kenite, a priest of Midian and, according to kabbalistic legend, he was the owner of a sapphire staff which had been given to Adam on the first Sabbath and passed on through the line of Enoch, Noah, Shem, Abraham, Isaac, Jacob and Joseph.

The staff is said to have had either the Divine Name or ten letters of unknown origin on it. Moses' affianced wife, Zipporah, told him the story of the rod and how it had rooted in Jethro's garden. Any potential suitor for her hand would have to pull it up which Moses was able to do: a precursor to the story of King Arthur and the sword in the stone.

This rod appeared later as Moses' and then Aaron's staff, then the scepter of King David. It was lost in the Ark of the Covenant after the purge of the First Temple. The staff is said to be a branch from the original Tree of Knowledge in the Garden of Eden.[72] This staff is associated with the feminine mystery tradition, too, in that the writer of the anonymous Holy Grail Writings, which inspired Malory's *Morte d'Arthur*, says that Eve pulled a twig and a leaf from the Tree of Knowledge and planted it as soon as she left Eden and set foot on Earth to remind her, and the rest of humanity, of the way back to the heavens. This young Tree of Knowledge was the sign outside Eden of how to find the way to the Tree of Life, the other tree that grew in the center of Paradise. This could be Wisdom's link between the Tree of Life and the Tree of Knowledge. We have eaten from the lesser tree; we cannot go back from that; we *do* discern good and evil. So we must retrace our footsteps to the one before we can aspire to the other – but perhaps they are both simply different aspects of the same tree.

From Eve's tree was cut a staff which was passed down through generations until it was given to Moses by Zipporah, who is said to be a priestess in the feminine line of the tradition. The 'sapphire' aspect of the staff refers to the sefirot of the Tree of Life and the ten letters represent the ten attributes of God.

Today, that staff of sapphires is reflected in a Christian Bishop's crook. It is also mentioned in the *Book of Mormon*. It is interesting that Jael the Kenite uses a wooden stave to kill Sisera; perhaps there is some lost link between her and Zipporah.

Deborah's place at Gevurah comes from her position as Judge of Israel. If she is 'the Lady of the Lightnings' this is even more appropriate. The archangelic presence at Gevurah at the level of Beriah is Khamael, known as 'The fire of God'.

Levels of Interpretation

Deborah and Jael's story is the stuff of legend; their place in a dominantly patriarchal society is notable, hence the Rabbis' haste either to cut them down or praise them. For us, Deborah is the lynchpin in that she is the voice of power and, if she did sit at the Grove of Asherah and she was a prophetess, she was a representative of the Goddess.

Allegorically, the story of Jael is not there to encourage us physically to kill an enemy but to examine where, in us, is the final point of resistance to whatever it is that we need to do, and to deal with it once and for all. At the level of the soul, this may often mean cutting ties, temporarily at least, with family and friends. Spiritual growth is unpopular to those who prefer the status quo, and the aspirant must keep their eye focused on where they want to go despite the calling of the tribe.

At the mental or emotional level, it is about seeing and eliminating habits or addictions which keep us from health or happiness. An example might be the elimination of Candida from our body. To cleanse the internal system of the harm caused by the overdevelopment of this yeast requires a complete repudiation of sugars and yeast-containing foods. Just one lapse during the process of treatment will nullify the whole effect. The principle of "just one sweet won't do any harm" is the principle of letting Sisera live to raise another army so that the war will begin again.

The story begins by telling us that when we lose our intent, our positivity and get bound up in politics or we focus on the idols of the time where we live – perhaps money, glamor or fame – we cut ourselves off from the Grace of God "the Lord gave them over to their enemies" (Judges 4:2).

At all levels, the story speaks of the power of "no" or "this stops here" or "we turn this around *now.*" It is all about boundaries. It also demonstrates the power of the Divine Feminine within us, and how important it is to acknowledge that power and handle it safely. This is the Dark Mother again – the element of the night, the darkness, the difficult decision, the possibility of deep pain or suffering if the cut is not swift and sure. It is no wonder that the sacred feminine has been seen as a threat or as an evil thing if it contains the power of life and death at this level.

Chapter Sixteen

The Surrender of the Soul – Hannah

Name: Hannah means 'grace'.

Hannah's story is told in the *First Book of Samuel*. She was a wife of Elkanah from the town of Ramah, believed to have been situated four or five miles from Jerusalem. Elkanah's other wife, Peninnah, had children, but Hannah was barren.

Midrash tells that Hannah was Elkanah's first wife and states that if a couple has been married for ten years without having any children, the husband is obliged to take another wife in order to fulfill the commandment to be fruitful and multiply.[73]

A different text states that Hannah is the one who decides that Elkanah should marry Peninnah, believing that if God sees that she has done right by her husband, he will remember her too.[74]

Elkanah continues to love Hannah but Peninnah is fertile, and rubs it in that Hannah is the lesser for her childlessness. Hannah *"wept, and did not eat"* (1 Samuel 1:7).

This is a direct parallel with the stories of Sarah and Hagar, and Leah and Rachel. However, despite her grief, Hannah responds in a very different way.

Her story begins as the family visits the city of Shiloh, the temporary home of the Ark of the Covenant and the Tabernacle. Hannah goes to the sacred place where the Ark is lodged to pray. *"And she was in bitterness of soul, and prayed unto the Lord, and wept sore"* (1 Samuel 1:10).

Hannah makes a vow that day, while Eli the priest watches her:

O Lord of hosts, if thou wilt indeed look on the affliction of thine handmaid, and remember me, and not forget thine handmaid, but wilt give unto thine handmaid a man child, then I will give him

unto the Lord all the days of his life, and there shall no razor come upon his head.
1 Samuel 1:11

The mention of the razor helps to define Hannah's vow. She is offering her son to be a Nazarite, as described in the *Book of Numbers*:

He shall separate from wine and strong drink, and shall drink no vinegar of wine, or vinegar of strong drink, neither shall he drink any liquor of grapes, nor eat moist grapes, or dried. All the days of his separation shall he eat nothing that is made of the vine tree, from the kernels even to the husk. All the days of the vow of his separation there shall no razor come upon his head: until the days be fulfilled, in which he separates unto the Lord, he shall be holy, and shall let the locks of the hair of his head grow. All the days that he separates unto the Lord he shall come at no dead body. He shall not make himself unclean for his father, or for his mother, for his brother, or for his sister, when they die: because the consecration of his God is upon his head. All the days of his separation he is holy unto the Lord.
Numbers 6:1

A Nazarite vow could be of any length of time from a few days to a lifetime. It's believed that St. Paul and many of the early Jewish Christians took this vow for a short while. However, Hannah vows her son for life.

How she prays is also of interest because she begins *"in great bitterness of soul"* but she *"spake in her heart; only her lips moved, but her voice was not heard."* The word translated as soul is *nefesh*, which in Kabbalah means the lower psyche, the part of us which is pulled by personal desires and social beliefs. But she speaks from her heart, *leb* in Hebrew, which implies *neshamah*, the higher will – the soul rather than the ego.

She also prays to *"the Lord of Hosts"*, being the first to do so in the Hebrew Bible ("hosts" referring to angels). The Rabbis put the following words into her mouth:

> There is a heavenly host and an earthly one. The heavenly host neither eat nor drink, are not fruitful and don't multiply, and do not die, but live forever. The earthly host eat and drink, are fruitful and multiply, and die. I do not know to which host I belong, whether to the heavenly host or the earthly one. If I am of the heavenly host, for I do not give birth, then I do not eat or drink and I shall not die, but live forever. But if I am of the earthly host, let me then eat and drink, give birth, and die.[75]

Eli thinks Hannah is drunk because she is mouthing words silently and he speaks harshly to her but, when she corrects him, he believes her and tells her to go in peace that God may grant her petition. This sounds like a priestly blessing. Hannah does so and the text says that she begins to eat again and her countenance is no longer sad.

The family returns to Ramah. Elkanah makes love to Hannah, *"the Lord remembered her"* (1 Samuel 1:19) and she gives birth to a son. She names him Samuel, Hebrew for 'his name is El'. El is one of the ten names of God used in the Hebrew Testament and refers to the Godly attribute of Mercy.

When Samuel is weaned (probably at about the age of three), Hannah takes him to the tabernacle together with an offering of three bullocks, some flour, and a bottle of wine. She meets up with Eli again and tells him how her prayer has been answered and, from then onwards, Samuel lives with the priests; Hannah visits him every year with clothing.

Hannah, too, has a song of praise (1 Samuel 2, 1–10). She gives birth to five other children and, according to Midrash, is merciful to Peninnah who becomes barren. Even worse, many of the younger wife's children die. Hannah prays that Peninnah may be spared her last two living children and the Lord hears her prayer.[76]

Samuel grows up under the tutelage of Eli and becomes a great prophet and priest.

Hannah and the Tree of Life

Hannah's story is placed within the Soul Triad, the space between the sefirot of Gevurah, Tiferet and Hesed. This is the aspect of the Tree of Life which understands that joy comes through service to God rather than service to the tribe. The Soul Triad is a vessel for receiving Divine Grace. It thrives on the use of our free will to overcome the tribal habits, niggles and beliefs of the lower triads and sefirot but it is, most importantly, the vessel for the Dew of Heaven; to access it we have to relax and allow the Grace of God rather than losing ourselves in the frets and bothers of our lower psyche.

The Soul Triad is where we feel free and confident of our true relationship with God, the Universe and our fellow men. Once Hannah has moved from the grief and stress of her *nefesh* which would block her from receiving Grace, her prayer from the heart is heard and granted. Eli's part in the story demonstrates that, while he may be talking the talk of a priest, he is not walking the walk. He is prepared to judge Hannah as a drunk rather than recognizing a genuine prayer from the passion of the soul.

Levels of Interpretation

It appears to be fairly clear that Hannah and Peninnah's story is a re-run of the griefs of the Matriarchs. But, this time, the oppressed and barren woman entreats the Lord directly. This shows spiritual growth within the feminine soul.

After Hannah's pilgrimage, her attitude changes before her condition does. She gives up her negative emotions and begins to live a normal life again, trusting that her prayer has been answered. This is a powerful message for us all; so often we pray or ask for help but then go on worrying about the problem. As the

'Hosts of Yahweh' are the angels, and the word angel means 'messenger', Hannah's confidence and comfort continues to send the positive prayer. Worry would be a negative prayer which also would be carried by the messengers of God, and might even cancel all the good of our initial prayer. This is a challenging lesson to learn, not least because we live in a modern society where we are deluged with negative thought and worst-case scenarios.

Hannah's message to us is trust that our prayers are heard. Mystically, she teaches us that the Divine and the feminine can work together in harmony. She does not curse Peninnah for her cruelty; rather she forgives her and prays for her when she is in distress. This story is the healing of the stories of the Matriarchs; the rising up of the feminine to embrace its Creator.

Chapter Seventeen

Into the Kingdom – Esther

Name: There are various translations of the name Esther. One is 'star', derived from the Indo-European root, *ster*. This is believed to refer back to the Persian Goddess Ishtar. As Ishtar is also associated with Ashratah, this is an important aspect of the story.

She is also named Hadassah, meaning 'Myrtle', an evergreen shrub used as an antiseptic tonic and for making perfume. Some sources say that the Hebrew root of Esther is *saiter*, meaning 'concealment' or 'hidden'.

Esther is the second of the two women in the Hebrew Testament who have their own book. The *Book of Ruth* is told in four chapters, one each for the four courts of the Temple and the Four Worlds of Jacob's Ladder. The Hebrew *Book of Esther* is told in ten chapters, one each for the sefirot on the Tree of Life.

However, there are two Biblical versions of Esther that we know of: the original Hebrew, known as the *Megillah*, and a six-part extension to the story in the later Greek *Septuagint*. The latter is fairly clearly an attempt to make more religious sense of the earlier story which, to the orthodox, contains some worrying aspects concerning Esther's marrying a non-Jew and the lack of mention of God in any way. It also contains what purport to be letters written by those taking part in the original story.

While it is important to refer to the Septuagint (and it contains some very valuable insights), the ten-chapter story of Esther is the one which would appear to point directly to the Divine Feminine. Esther herself is the reflection of God in this story. She comes "into the Kingdom" – the Kingdom of God – and offers her life in her bid to become the savior of her people.

The Septuagint also contains a verse expressing Esther's extreme distaste for having to marry a non-Jewish man; this issue is not addressed in the Hebrew Testament but it is backed up by extensive commentary in Midrash in order to try and explain Esther's perceived transgressions in marrying the King of Persia, seducing him, not eating *kosher* food and – in one outrageous claim – being an adulteress.

The story begins with a 180-day long party given by the King of Persia, Ahasuerus (also known as Artaxerxes), in the city of Shushan at the time of the Babylonian exile. This event climaxes with a seven-day feast with the king entertaining the men and his queen, Vashti, entertaining the women. During the feast the king commands his seven chamberlains to bring the queen before his guests in her royal crown. He wants to show off her beauty to them.

Vashti refuses to come. It's worth noting here that in most societies in those days, including the Jewish ones, the only women who appeared at an all-male party would be dancers or prostitutes, and the king's summons directly contravened the law. This may excuse Vashti's behavior.

However, Ahasuerus is angry and asks the seven princes of the provinces what he should do (this immediately tells us that while he may be a strong warrior, he is a weak king).

The princes are horrified by what has happened, terrified that this feminine defiance may spread and they decree that Vashti must be banished.

For this deed of the queen shall come abroad unto all women, so that they shall despise their husbands in their eyes, when it shall be reported, The king Ahasuerus commanded Vashti the queen to be brought in before him, but she came not. Likewise shall the ladies of Persia and Media say this day unto all the king's princes, which have heard of the deed of the queen. Thus shall there arise too much contempt and wrath.
Esther 1:17–18

The king does as they insist and even:

> sent letters into all the king's provinces, into every province according to the writing thereof, and to every people after their language, that every man should bear rule in his own house, and that it should be published according to the language of every people. Esther 1:22

So we know, very clearly from the start, where we stand on the position of men and women in this time.

However, a new queen is needed in order to ensure the succession and the king's ministers decide that *"fair young virgins"* (Esther 2:2) should be selected from throughout Persia and brought to the harem to be introduced to the king, who will decide which one should become his queen. A decree goes out and women flock to a series of beauty contests.

In Chapter Two we are introduced to Esther, who is a Hebrew girl living in the city of Shushan. She is an orphan: the adopted daughter and either the niece or cousin of a man named Mordecai.

For the beauty of Esther's story to unfold we will stay with the Hebrew for the moment and examine the alternatives later.

Esther is *"a maid who was fair and beautiful"* (Esther 2:7) and she is chosen to be one of the women to be set before the king as a potential new wife. Each of these will spend an evening with the king in turn, and then either be declared the new queen or sent to the harem.

It is made clear that Esther is neither a proud woman nor a vain one. When it is her turn she delights the king – who may, by then, be fed up to the back teeth with perfumes and preening – and he declares her to be his new queen.

Mordecai charges Esther not to reveal her Jewish origin so when she and the king are married, nobody knows of her religion. Mordecai himself begins to spend time every day outside the king's gate to enquire how the new queen might be. One day, while he is there, he overhears a plot to kill Ahasuerus; he lets Esther know and she warns the king, also telling him the name of the man who has saved him. The plot is foiled.

Ahasuerus has a favored, highly-promoted servant, Haman, who is from one of the tribes dispossessed by the Hebrews when they came to the Promised Land. He hates the Hebrews and his anger is exacerbated each day when he sees Mordecai sitting at the gate waiting for news of Esther. This is because Mordecai refuses to honor him even though the king has decreed that all men must bow to Haman.

Haman's anger is such that he decides to make the king exterminate the Jews throughout his empire. He justifies the action by saying that they keep themselves apart from the king's laws and says he needs money to pay those who will destroy them. Ahasuerus believes him. "*And the king said unto Haman, The silver is given to thee, the people also, to do with them as it seemeth good to thee*" (Esther 3:11). Ahasuerus doesn't really care; he just wants a quiet life.

Edicts are posted throughout Persia that the Jews are to be killed and all their goods seized on one particular day.

Mordecai hears the news and goes to the gate of the palace in sackcloth and ashes, lamenting; Esther hears of this and sends a servant to know what is wrong and he sends her a message back together with a copy of the decree, charging her to go to the king to save them.

This is the message that Esther sends back:

All the king's servants, and the people of the king's provinces, do know, that whosoever, whether man or woman, shall come unto the king into the inner court, who is not called, there is one law of his to put him to death, except such to whom the king shall hold out the golden scepter, that he may live: but I have not been called to come

in unto the king these thirty days.
Esther 4:11

Esther and the king have been married for five years with, as yet, no child. She has not seen her husband for thirty days which indicates a general estrangement. If Midrash is to be believed, Esther is a reluctant wife. A more likely alternative is that she has not found it easy to move from poor Jewess to Persian Queen – Cinderella marrying the prince is only the start of the story. It may well be that she has disappointed her husband in more ways than one by not conceiving.

Whatever the reason, at the moment when it matters most, Esther is not in any powerful position of influence to save the Jews and, as she has not even revealed that she herself is a Jewess, even if she could approach the king, this last-minute revelation would be unlikely to be viewed sympathetically.

Mordecai sends back to her this:

Think not with thyself that thou shalt escape in the king's house, more than all the Jews. For if thou altogether holdest thy peace at this time, then shall there enlargement and deliverance arise to the Jews from another place; but thou and thy father's house shall be destroyed: and who knoweth whether thou art come to the kingdom for such a time as this?
Esther 4:13

The simplest interpretation of the phrase 'into the kingdom' would be 'become queen' but the world for kingdom is *Malkhut*, the name of the sefira in the Divine World of Azilut that is the place of the Shekhinah. This same sefira is known as 'the kingdom of God'.

Mordecai is reminding Esther not only that she has a duty to try and save her people, but also that she is divinely appointed to be where she is; this is her sacred destiny.

Esther hears him and requests that he and the people pray and fast for her for three days and then she will go to the king. *"And if I die, I die"* (Esther 4:14).

On the third day, according to most English translations of the Hebrew Testament, Esther puts on her royal apparel or her crown before going before the king. But the Hebrew is clear: she puts on her *Malkhut*; she comes into her own Divine essence. She presents herself as Shekhinah on Earth.

In the Septuagint it says: *"The little fountain which grew into a river and was turned into a light and into the sun and abounded into many waters, is Esther."* (Mordecai's dream, Esther 10:6.)

Even so, Esther must have gone before the king uncertain of her fate – this is a man who has already rid himself of one troublesome wife who refused to obey him but, when Ahasuerus sees her,

> she obtained favor in his sight: and the king held out to Esther the golden scepter that was in his hand. So Esther drew near, and touched the top of the scepter. Then said the king unto her, 'What wilt thou, queen Esther? And what is thy request? It shall be even given thee to the half of the kingdom.'
> Esther 5:2

This is either a man in love who is pleased to see his wife after a long estrangement or a king who sees a true queen. To offer half your kingdom to someone who has just broken the law is not a normal response.

That Esther either *is* or *has* Wisdom is clear. She does not pour out her petition; that would mean letting go of her power of ascendency and appearing to be seeking only help. Instead, as a true queen, simply and with great dignity she invites the king and Haman to dinner.

Haman, remember, is the mortal enemy of the Jews. By all accounts it would have been easier for Esther to invite only her husband. However, she is extending a respect to the king's greatest courtier that Mordecai was unable to do.

The evening is a success and, at the end of it, Ahasuerus asks Esther what her petition may be. Again, Esther is Wisdom. She says nothing about the threat to the Jews but asks for the two men to return for another banquet the following night. No scholarly explanation is given anywhere for this delay;[77] but Esther is acting with great prudence. That night two things happen which are of vital importance. Despite the honor of dining alone with the king and queen, Haman cannot stop thinking about the disrespect that Mordecai is showing to him every day. On his wife's advice he builds a gallows, fifty cubits high, and sets off to tell the king that Mordecai should be hanged on it. Meanwhile, Ahasuerus cannot sleep and sends for a slave to read to him. The text that is chosen is the one telling how Mordecai uncovered the plot against Ahasuerus' life. The king asks what honors were given to the man who saved him and discovers that nothing whatsoever was done; the underlying implication being that Haman was responsible for that lack of respect.

There follows a strange vignette of Ahasuerus sending for Haman and asking him what should be done for someone whom the king would delight to honor. Haman thinks the king is referring to him and shows his true colors. He says:

> Let the royal apparel be brought which the king useth to wear, and the horse that the king rideth upon, and the crown royal which is set upon his head: And let this apparel and horse be delivered to the hand of one of the king's most noble princes, that they may array the man withal whom the king delighteth to honor, and bring him on horseback through the street of the city, and proclaim before him, Thus shall it be done to the man whom the king delighteth to honor. Esther 6:8-9

In modern terminology, this is colossal cheek and it shows the inflated size of Haman's ego.

The king wrong-foots him cleverly and tells him to do all that he has suggested to Mordecai, in return for the great service that the Jew has given, and Haman, in full humiliation, has to do just that. Does the king suggest this to test him? Has he realized the failings of his favorite? If so, then Esther's decision to wait another day before petitioning him has paid off in a very powerful way.

That night, at the second banquet, the king asks his wife again what her petition might be, saying that he would grant it, even if it were for half the kingdom.

> *Then Esther the queen answered and said, 'If I have found favor in thy sight, O king, and if it please the king, let my life be given me at my petition, and my people at my request: For we are sold, I and my people, to be destroyed, to be slain, and to perish'... Then the king Ahasuerus answered and said unto Esther the queen, 'Who is he, and where is he, that durst presume in his heart to do so?'*
> Esther 7:3–5

This is the poetry of the Hebrew Testament at its best; it tells us so clearly that whatever may have happened between them, Ahasuerus and his queen are now capable of becoming one; we could even see it as Yahweh and Asherah reunited to stand together against a common enemy.

The king may be reunited with the queen but Ahasuerus the man, the weaker aspect, goes out into the garden for some air, realizing that he has to choose between queen and favorite, and Haman throws himself on Esther to beg for mercy. This is misinterpreted – perhaps deliberately – by Ahasuerus who accuses him of attacking the queen or, perhaps, attempting to rape her. The decision is made and Haman is hanged on the special gallows that he had prepared for Mordecai.

The rest of the book involves Esther telling the king that

Mordecai is her uncle and the three of them working together to solve the problem of the attack against the Jews. As the original decree permitted all the Persian people to attack them, not just an army, the solution is to grant the Jews permission to retaliate. There is a battle but the Jews prevail and Mordecai is given Haman's position and all his possessions. Esther and Ahasuerus live happily ever after.

For Midrash, the abiding problem throughout the story is how Esther, a Jewish woman, could marry outside the tribe. This is justified because it is only by being married to the king that Esther could stop the massacre, but it is obviously a painful subject for the Rabbis.

The Talmud attacks the issue further by stating that Esther was Mordecai's wife rather than his adopted daughter.[78] This changes the whole tenet of the story. One Midrash claims that Esther was over 40 years old; another says she was 80.[79]

Both are in direct opposition to the Hebrew text which says, clearly, that the Esther who was chosen to be one of the women to be set before the king as a potential new wife was a maid who was fair and beautiful. Logic would decree that this is far more likely than a middle-aged or elderly married woman being selected even if she were pretending to be a virgin!

The Rabbis also believed that Esther was compelled to marry Ahasuerus against her will and that she refused to have sex with him.[80] Moreover, she continued to live with Mordecai, at the same time that she was married to Ahasuerus.[81] Both these claims are palpably ridiculous. Even if Ahasuerus might have tolerated a second wife who despised or defied him, he would not have spared her when she came to the inner court. And Mordecai would never have had to sit in the gate to find out how Esther might be if she were still living with him.

Whatever had happened between them, Ahasuerus obviously had a regard for his queen. And in the Septuagint, where most of Esther's story is repeated twice with additions in the second part, there is a beautiful paragraph where Esther speaks to the king after he has raised the scepter to her when she comes to him.

I saw thee, my lord, as an angel of God: and my heart was troubled for fear of thy majesty. For thou, my lord, art very admirable; and thy face is full of graces.
Esther 15:17–18

It is possible that Esther and Ahasuerus loved each other as fallible humans and came out of their respective tribes and into the Kingdom together.

Esther and the Tree of Life

Esther is placed at Hesed, the sefira of mercy and loving kindness. There is a tradition within Kabbalah that the Tree of Life can be pulled straight to become the central column of Jacob's Ladder. If that is done, the sefira of Hesed becomes the Malkhut of the Divine World of Azilut; the Kingdom of God and the abode of Shekhinah; the place of the Messiah.

There are also significant repetitions of the numbers seven and ten within the book. The seven lower sefirot of the Tree (from Malkhut to Hesed) are said to reflect everyday life in the physical World; the top three are known as the Supernal Triad, the reflections of God. When seven is referred to, it will indicate a worldly cycle, such as the seven days in a week; and when ten is referred to, it is a complete cycle reflecting a clear good or a distinct evil.

On the seventh day of the great feast, Ahasuerus tells his seven chamberlains to fetch Vashti the queen, and the seven princes at the feast encourage him to dismiss her.

Esther's story is told in ten chapters and she goes before the king in the tenth month after she is taken into the harem, implying that she is fully perfected. Ahasuerus is in the seventh year of his reign when he meets her. When she goes before him again to plead for her people, she fasts for three days; the implication being that she has to re-purify herself; to lift herself consciously from the seven lower sefirot back up to the Supernal Triad.

What seals Esther's place at Hesed is her behavior to Haman, the man who is the greatest enemy of both her and her people. At this level of consciousness she can and does forgive him by inviting him to dine with her and the King. Hesed is the sefira of true unconditional love. This is the level from which Jesus said *"Father, forgive them; they know not what they do"* (Luke 23:34).

She is also willing to give her life in order to try and save her people. *"No one has greater spiritual love than this: that they would offer their life for those they care for"* (John 15:13, my translation).

Haman is said later in the text to have had ten sons, all of whom are also hanged. This would be an indication of his complete evil intention.

There is also an interesting use of colors when Mordecai is lifted to Haman's position:

> *And Mordecai went out from the presence of the king in royal apparel of blue and white, and with a great crown of gold, and with a garment of fine linen and purple: and the city of Shushan rejoiced and was glad.*
> Esther 8:15

Exodus 36:1 tells us that purple, blue and white are the three colors of the three inner courts of the Hebrew Tabernacle; these are also the three higher Worlds of Jacob's Ladder. Ahasuerus' feast included awnings in the colors of red, purple, blue and white, all four colors of the tabernacle.

Levels of Interpretation

The story of Esther, Mordecai and Haman is the basis for the Jewish festival of Purim which is celebrated each spring on the

14th day of the month of Adar (usually in March). It is a festival where celebration is emphasized including strong drink and plenty of it. Esther's story is very unusual in that it is also contained in the writings of the Jewish historian, Josephus.[82]

The fact that the book does not refer to God in its Hebrew version is believed to be why Esther is the only book of the testament that was not found among the Dead Sea Scrolls.

Esther's descendants are said to be the founders of the rebuilding of the Temple after the Babylonian exile.

The story is not only about how hard it can be to step up and leave the tribe, but how important it is to do so. It is as much about Mordecai as about Esther; who knows, if he had been willing to bow to Haman (as the law decreed), whether the massacre would even have been planned? In Exodus 32:9 the Lord calls the Jews "a stiff-necked people" and Mordecai is just that. He is as willing as Haman to continue in a tribal war. Esther, on the other hand, is willing, figuratively at least, to bow to Haman by inviting him to dinner with her and the king.

Esther is told by Mordecai not to reveal that she is a Jewess. Had she told the king of her faith at the start, the story would, again, have been different. However, many of the great stories of the world, from the classic nursery rhymes to the 21st century Harry Potter, require the hero to hold back some information for the plot to be able to unfold.

What Esther has to learn is how to be a queen. For us, the lesson is twofold. Firstly, how to become our true selves whatever the tribe may think of us. To seek our destiny where God calls us, and not through repeating the errors of those who have gone before. Also, how to come into the Kingdom ourselves; how to ensure that where we stand is holy ground; to become the emissary of God on Earth. We have to be willing to give our life for that goal, our life meaning the everyday comfort of tribal consciousness.

She also has to be able to forgive; to release the belief that

Haman's tribal vindictiveness can harm her and to allow God to dissolve the problem. And the forgiveness must extend to her husband's co-operation with the edict – possibly an even worse action given that he had no personal opinion about the Jews and allowed a potential holocaust to be organized on Haman's word.

We find forgiveness the hardest thing. It is not supported by our modern-day culture of sharing and celebrating wounds. But our anger is far more destructive to us than it is to those who would harm us. We give them more power with our hatred and, even more tragically, stand in the way of the solution.

Just as Hannah sent her plea to the Lord and then let go of her problem, Esther releases all opinions and simply offers love. She, Hannah, Jael and Deborah all demonstrate the power of the human soul to detach from the problem and receive the healing.

Esther's story takes place during the Babylonian exile after the purging of the Temple. Metaphysically, Esther herself is a representative of the Queen of Heaven in exile with her people, offering her life in order to bring them to salvation.

Chapter Eighteen

The Women and the Ten Commandments

The Ten Commandments of the Hebrew Testament can also be linked with the women placed on the ten sefirot of the Tree of Life (fig. 4, fig. 5). Kabbalah teaches that many of the commandments have a deeper meaning than just the literal one.

The Commandments descend from Keter to Malkhut on the Tree of Life: the first three being concerned with our relationship with God and the other seven (below the separation of Daat – Knowledge) to do with how we live in the everyday world.

The Commandments begin at the top of the Tree in the Supernal Triad of Binah, Keter and Hokhmah and drop down along a lightning flash, zigzagging from one side of the Tree to the other all the way down to Malkhut. The Commandments are first given in Exodus Chapter 20, are repeated after the incident of the Golden Calf and again when the Israelites are about to reach the Promised Land.

The First Commandment is:

I am the Lord thy God, which have brought thee out of the land of Egypt, out of the house of bondage. Thou shalt have no other gods before me [before my face].

This commandment is placed at Keter. It tells us clearly that other gods exist and are being worshipped. For the modern age, this may refer to other kinds of idols that we revere, whether it is a way of life, money, glamor or fame. The reference to bringing us out of Egypt, out of bondage, means that if we put anything in our life before our own direct relationship with God we are returning to the slavery of a world which binds us by social convention or rules. Only by putting God first can we remain free of the slavery of the world's desires.

It is not an easy commandment and may be misinterpreted to mean we should put our religion before anything else. But the instruction is clear; it is about our own, individual relationship with God, and for many of us there has to be much unraveling of inbuilt belief before we can take the hand of the Holy One.

This commandment is not related to a particular woman within the Bible – or to any man. It is about every one of us and our communion with who and what we believe God to be. It does not say that we may not feel passionate about material things or our beliefs, but that they should not be our be-all and end-all. The Biblical system of tithing puts this very clearly in its injunction to give first to God, then to celebration and then to others. Celebration (including feasting and enjoying attractive things) is not forbidden; in fact it is encouraged. But only after we have focused on the Source first. That way we can be guided to make clear and wise decisions.

The Second Commandment is:

Thou shalt not make unto thee any graven image, or any likeness of any thing that is in heaven above, or that is in the earth beneath, or that is in the water under the earth: Thou shalt not bow down thyself to them, nor serve them: for I the Lord thy God am a jealous God, visiting the iniquity of the fathers upon the children unto the third and fourth [generation] of them that hate me; And shewing mercy unto thousands of them that love me, and keep my commandments.

This Commandment is placed at Hokhmah. It is an extension of the first commandment but its focus is on the 'graven image' which means something set in stone. It does not mean that we must make no pictures of anything in heaven, the water or the earth, just that we must not judge one particular image as the only one which is correct. If we believe that there is only one illustration that is right, then any other will be judged to be wrong – or even evil. We break this commandment every time a pedigree horse or dog is rejected because it does not conform to the correct specifications of a breeder's club or when we believe that God is a grey-bearded old man in the sky rather than all-embracing, indefinable spirit.

The 'jealousy' of God refers to 'jealous of principle' in that the law is exact and will be enacted: whatever we judge will be returned to us in judgment. Should we become mired with hatred for anything (for God created all) then that hatred will be reflected back to us. The word 'generation' is missing in the testament and has been added in to make better exoteric sense. If we demonstrate love and mercy, those too will be reflected back to us. It makes logical sense that the same events or situations would happen to our children and grandchildren, as we are the ones who teach them what to believe and how to behave. They then have our example as a graven image and may repeat our mistakes.

Adam is placed here in the *Zohar* and in many kabbalistic traditions, and this is appropriate both because Hokhmah is at the head of the masculine pillar of the Tree of Life, and because he and Eve were the first to judge right and wrong. But for our story, the aspect of creation which fits this commandment is Lilith.

Lilith's story is so bound in tradition as being about the evil within the feminine that it inspires harsh reactions within us whichever view we take. In this book I have tried to take Lilith away from the graven image. She never existed and yet she is set in stone. For traditionalists she is the original disobedient and rebellious woman; for feminists she is a heroine and an icon of liberation.

And if she did refuse to bow to or lie below Adam then she too believed in a graven image: that to go below, to surrender, to receive, made her lesser. That is not to say that a woman should submit to a man – but that all humanity should be willing to surrender power (or control) where it is appropriate. And part of that surrender includes sharing our knowledge and our kindness with others. Some days it's fine to be top dog, to be the one who gives, who decides and who is most powerful; and on other days it's important to be the receptive vessel, to allow others to serve us, give to us or advise us. It is all in the flexibility of allowing perceptions to change and evolve as we do.

The Third Commandment is:

Thou shalt not take the name of the LORD thy God in vain; for the LORD will not hold him guiltless that taketh his name in vain.

This Commandment is placed at Binah. At the literal level, it is about being respectful and not throwing any of the names of God around in profanity. But at a deeper level it is much more powerful. The name of God is 'I Am'. So to take the name of God in vain is to misuse the 'I Am' as in saying: "I am worthless; I am wrong; I am stupid; I am not good enough." Likewise, we misuse it when we do not take responsibility. This extends beyond the simple 'I am' to 'I did', 'I will' and the word 'yes'. It is also taking it in vain if we promise to do something and do not fulfill our promise. It is perfectly allowable to ask to be released from a promise but not simply to walk away from it as though it had never been made.

Eve is the expression of this commandment because she made the first choice. To make a choice you have to see yourself as separate: outside of a situation. If you are deeply involved in an egoic matter, very few choices can be made as every circumstance appears to be a graven image of what you 'should' do. Eve broke away from everything known before in the Garden of Eden. Had she then taken responsibility for it, she would have kept the commandment even though she disobeyed God's instruction. There would have been honor in the owning up to having dared to be different.

The Fourth Commandment is:

Remember the Sabbath day, to keep it holy. Six days shalt thou labor, and do all thy work: But the seventh day is the Sabbath of the Lord thy God: in it thou shalt not do any work, thou, nor thy son, nor thy daughter, thy manservant, nor thy maidservant, nor thy cattle, nor thy stranger that is within thy gates: For in six days the Lord made heaven and earth, the sea, and all that in them is, and rested the seventh day: wherefore the Lord blessed the Sabbath day, and hallowed it.

This commandment is placed at Hesed. It is interesting that its wording is slightly inaccurate as Genesis clearly states that God (Elohim) created the world, not the Lord (Yahweh). However, it's a sensible commandment for the first of the laws for the everyday world. It is simply telling us to get some rest and relaxation. To keep something holy means to make it sacred – special. In our modern world of rush and continual communication, very few people take a day away from some aspect of work, technology or from the mundanity of everyday life. Holidays were once holy days… and we all know the refreshment of a real holiday. The commandment just tells us to take time out once a week; not to be at the beck and call of the everyday world. It is when we go within that we are filled. If we do not go within, all too often we go without.

Esther is the personification of this commandment because she paused; she waited; she took time out for sanctification and for calm and for courage. When she knew that she must go before the king and risk her life, she prepared herself with fasting and asked Mordecai to get her people to do the same. At the level of the psyche, fasting does not necessarily mean not eating; it refers to purging ourselves of any kind of negativity. In Esther's case that would have been fear and self-doubt. It is often only when we step back from a problem that the answer appears. If we fast from the everyday thoughts and assumptions, we will create a space for the Holy One to communicate with us and we will hear the Divine Voice.

Esther also waits after the first evening when Ahasuerus asks for her petition. Most of us would have rushed in with our demand but Esther knew that the time was not yet right. A Sabbath is a time of reflection, of self-development, of self-worth. It is beautifully summed up by this quotation (author unknown):

If, as Herod, we fill our lives with things, and again with things; if we consider ourselves so unimportant that we must fill every moment of our lives with action, when will we have the time to make the long, slow journey across the desert as did the Magi?

Or sit and watch the stars, as did the shepherds? Or brood over the coming of the child, as did Mary? For each one of us, there is a desert to travel. A star to discover.

And a being within us to bring to life.[83]

The Fifth Commandment is:

Honor thy father and thy mother: that thy days may be long upon the land which the LORD thy God giveth thee.

This commandment is placed at Gevurah. Literally it does refer to our parents. We must respect their beliefs and origins and understand their motivations, based on all that they have experienced, but it does not say that we must like them, obey them nor even follow their example. It also means to honor the different ways that the masculine and feminine worship and work – which is the foundation of this book. To deny the feminine is to deny part of God. Neither masculine nor feminine is greater than the other. *"Hear the instruction of thy father, and forsake not the law of thy mother"* (Proverbs 1:8).

Allegorically and spiritually, however, it asks us to honor the Sacred Masculine and the Divine Feminine at all levels. In Pagan traditions, our father is the sky god and our mother the earth, so it is an injunction to observe the beauty and glory of the stars, and also to protect and conserve the planet on which we live.

It also refers to whatever spiritual tradition into which we were born. We don't have to follow it but it is incumbent upon us to investigate the truth within it; to find the honor there rather than accepting what we are told or rejecting it out of hand.

Deborah represents this commandment as she counterbalances the masculine heritage of power in Israel. Her story, and that of Jael, represents the balance of masculine battle and feminine martial art in ending a long-running war. Interestingly, the Hebrew word translated as 'honor' is *kabad* which has a primary meaning of 'weighty' or 'heavy'. A tradition is a heavy thing; it has to be treated with respect but it does not have to be followed blindly when there is a need for new growth. It is also hard work. Jael honored the need for peace and was willing to carry out the deed that would ensure it. That cannot have been easy. In Samurai culture she honored Sisera by executing him cleanly rather than handing him over to the Hebrew army where his death would not have been so swift.

It is important to mention here the concept of 'honor killing' which is the negative side of this commandment and *not* what Jael did. There is no honor in killing someone who wishes peacefully to leave your tradition, faith or religion, and embrace a new way of life.

The Sixth Commandment is:

Thou shalt not commit murder.

This commandment is placed at Tiferet. It is not 'thou shalt not kill'. The Hebrew word *ratsach* refers to an intention to destroy, and is used with reference to other human beings. It does not refer to accidental killing, nor to the killing of animals. In the ancient law of the Hebrews it is acceptable to kill in self-defense or to save others, and it is permissible to kill animals to eat or to ensure the survival of yourself, others or of your crops or flocks. It is even permissible for a woman to have an abortion if her mental health or her life is in danger.[84]

However, the kabbalistic interpretation of this commandment extends to murder of the soul or psyche. It is murder to destroy somebody else's dreams or their desire to explore the world for themselves (see 'honor killing' above). It is spiritual murder to destroy your own life for the sake of others. Again, this is not an easy commandment; we are taught that to give and to care for others is to be a virtuous person. But if you have to sacrifice your own spiritual growth to care for one who does not wish to grow then it may be balm to the vegetable level but suicide to the human soul.

Is it murder to the other to walk away from them? No. If your soul seeks enlightenment and you move on, another will come to take your place and this will be someone who is better suited to the role of carer than you may be with your restless heart.

Ruth embodies all that is positive in this commandment in that having learnt from Naomi about the one God and observed her mother-in-law's faith, she chose to step out and step up for the sake of her own soul. It is easy for us today to dismiss what a huge undertaking that was. Had Ruth stayed behind with Orpah and reintegrated into life in Moab, her soul and spirit would have withered.

The Seventh Commandment is:

Thou shalt not commit adultery.

This commandment is placed at Nezah.

To adulterate is to add something to a mix which makes the original impure or destroys it. In most marriages, the addition of a lover is destructive; in a few it might enhance the original relationship. If it enhances, then it is not adulterous. On the other hand, a couple who have ceased to love each other but who stay together may be committing adultery if they have brought indifference or hatred into something which was once pure.

Rachel may have been Jacob's first love but, by marrying him after her sister, she brought adultery into the marriage. Neither she nor Leah could be at peace with the other sister. It could be said that Rachel also committed adultery by using the mandrakes or stealing the teraphim – but if either of those was instrumental in helping her to achieve her heart's desire and become pregnant, then they enhanced her life and her marriage rather than hurt them. Was that adultery against God? Conventional religion would say it was. But it would be a poor god which objected to a woman's happiness and, if we worship the kind of god who wishes us unhappiness, that could be considered an adulterous relationship too.

The Eighth Commandment is:

Thou shalt not steal.

This commandment is placed at Hod.

Hod is also known as the place of the trickster or the scoundrel. It is the sefira of cleverness and sleight-of-hand. Leah is the personification of Hod for she stole Jacob from Rachel. To steal from another is to believe that you have less than they do, and is a denial of any kind of abundance. Leah could not trust that she would marry a man who wanted her – or perhaps any man at all. But no theft has a positive consequence for the thief, for there can be no feeling of true self-worth in the action nor in its consequences.

The Ninth Commandment is:

Thou shalt not bear false witness against thy neighbor.

This commandment is placed at Yesod.

To bear false witness is to tell an untruth whether it's an outright intention to deceive, or perpetrating a juicy piece of gossip which may or may not be true. Much of what we talk about in the media-driven world is speculation rather than fact. It is also bearing false witness to say that something is better than it is, whether that is to cover up our own inadequacies, or to promote an event or a product that does not live up to its advertising.

Rebekah bore false witness when she encouraged and assisted Jacob to deceive his father. It was also false witness that a woman who had previously communicated directly with the Lord turned away from that source of inspiration, taking control for her own sake.

The Tenth Commandment is:

Thou shalt not covet thy neighbor's house, thou shalt not covet thy neighbor's wife, nor his manservant, nor his maidservant, nor his ox, nor his ass, nor any thing that is thy neighbor's.

This commandment is placed at Malkhut.

For most of us this is one of the hardest commandments to keep; it seems quite natural to envy the wealth, happiness or health of another who seems to be better or richer than us. But from envy springs the desire to break nearly every other commandment. It does not mean that we should not aspire – to create and to grow are essential human attributes – it means that we must not compare ourselves with others. Comparisons are always odious. Either we think we are better or worse than the other, and this is the epitome of the issue around eating from the Tree of Knowledge. We judge the possession, or not, of some things as being good or bad.

The modern world is one of acquisition and status through things. We are encouraged to envy so that we too will purchase and acquire. But when we focus on what another has rather than on our own relationship with the Divine, we close the door to our own greater good – the abundance of God given to us in a perfect way in the perfect time.

Sarah reflects this commandment. She tried to ensure that her husband would have a child to become the father of a nation but her action led to terrible feelings of envy and anger. Like many of us, she found it almost impossible to trust that God would bring her own good in the right time. It had to be now and it had to be under her control.

The message of all the commandments is to trust that God loves us and will help and guide us. A wise man once said that we are given threescore years and ten because by the end of them, we can keep all Ten Commandments. If that is so, perhaps all the women of the Hebrew Testament who lived to a good age eventually found peace and happiness. I do hope so.

Conclusion

We began with the breath of God into the androgynous human being, Adamah. This is the point of conception of the human soul and its links to the higher Worlds. From the beginning we were given free will; we can choose to accept Grace in our lives or we can turn away believing that we can handle everything ourselves.

If we are to believe the legend of Lilith, humanity turned away. But this story is not in the Bible; it dates from the time of the Babylonian exile so it is far more likely to be what is known as 'an apologetic' – a defense against accusations – for the purging of the Divine Feminine from the First Temple. If the feminine were corrupt, apostate, abominable, then it was right that she should be demonstrated to have turned away from the true God herself and it was appropriate for humanity also to reject her.

The story was necessary because the narrative of Eve was commonly believed to take place in the physical World; Eve was a human being, not a potential goddess. Her behavior was seen as a reflection of the behaviors of woman as a whole but, as victim to Lilith's attacks on her children, she could be seen as much the injured party as the perpetrator. The divine Valkyrie who flew away from God and her husband must be rejected and feared by women as much as by men.

From there is the fall (or perhaps more accurately the descent) into matter and the beginning of the journey back to the Godhead. The Tree of Knowledge is shown on the kabbalistic diagram of the Tree of Life as the non-sefira of Daat. Daat is known as the place of Knowledge; the linking point between different levels of Jacob's Ladder and, in the Yeziratic World, the long dark night of the soul between the psyche and spirit. To become holy, perfected and to touch the hem of the Divine garment, we have to let go of our opinions of what is good and what is bad and simply to accept what is. Only in doing that can we love unconditionally. We have to transcend Knowledge into Understanding and Wisdom.

For Sarah and Hagar, the first women to begin the re-ascent of the Tree, there was Divine help even if it seemed to be a long time coming. Angels worked on their behalf; God remembered Sarah and the Lord gave her a son. Hagar was protected and sent home when she ran away and, when her son's behavior provoked Sarah again, she was supported by God who opened her eyes so she saw a life-giving well of water. The Elohim loved both women and understood them.

Even so, the enmity between Sarah and Hagar may well have been the origins of the Arab-Israeli conflict that we still see in the world today.

Rebekah chose to see herself as the agent of the Lord in making manifest His prediction that Jacob would be the chosen one to succeed Isaac. Perhaps she was the agent but her method of achieving the goal did not involve prayer or listening for guidance as to whether her plan was an appropriate one. She was entirely willful in taking control, and the consequences were deeply distressing. She lost the son she loved, as well as the trust of her husband, and she incurred the enmity of the son and his foreign wives with whom she would have to live for the rest of her life.

Esau and Jacob made up their quarrel once Jacob returned to the old land willing to take the consequences of his action, even if Esau should kill him. Today, the Palestinians see the Israelis as exiles who have returned without that essential humility while Israel (harking back to Sarah) sees the Palestinians as a lesser people trying to steal its God-given land.

Jacob wrestled with God for all of his life but his wives, Leah and Rachel, wrestled only with each other over who should possess magical mandrakes and who will get to sleep with him. They may have been the mothers of the twelve tribes of Israel, but the one daughter they would have raised between them to learn from their mistakes had no strength or support of any kind. Leah did not speak up for her daughter and Rachel did not speak up for her niece.

Miriam did speak up – mostly to good effect. This was a feisty woman who had her own opinions and was not afraid to voice them and who was willing to take risks. With this came the well of living water that followed the Israelites in the desert for as long as she lived. Miriam was an embodiment of the Divine Feminine on Earth; in essence a part of the Tabernacle and perhaps also its priestess. As Moses was cast into living water and rescued by the princess of Egypt, the princess too represents the Divine. Two different tribes worked together for a higher purpose and this is the hidden wisdom, the secret message of healing throughout the Hebrew Testament.

Miriam was not perfect; she dipped back into the consciousness of the lower psyche and spoke out against Moses' foreign wife. The consequences were severe. The nearer we stand to God's Grace, the further and faster we fall if we transgress a higher law. But Miriam was loved, and Moses spoke to the Lord on her behalf that she be healed.

Dinah's story could have been similar to Esther's: she was loved by royalty but, in her case, the psyches of her family could not let her go; could not see that this would be an enhancement to the tribe and chose war instead.

Rahab chose to save herself and her family which led her to change tribes. But she was impressed by the Hebrew God and His powers, as was Ruth. While Rahab chose safety, Ruth chose adventure and the possibility of poverty because of the strength of her faith – which rewarded her a hundredfold.

Deborah and Jael were willing to fight for what they believed in. For Deborah, it was victory for her people; for Jael it was victory for peace.

Esther had to learn to accept that her destiny was to be a

queen which meant great responsibility. She offered her life for her people and brought down the Divine Feminine to earth to be reunited with the Divine Masculine. She came *"into the Kingdom."*

Every one of these women is within us; we are as brave and as weak as they are. Each woman has a lesson to teach us and each woman carries the Divine within her heart. It may not show in all these stories but it is there in potential. At worst, we can learn from their errors, their attempts to control the outcome; at best we can be inspired by their communion with God and their willingness to stand on Holy Ground.

Today, whether we are male or female, we can step up to acknowledge that the Divine Feminine is within us too. She is our mother, our wife and our sister, ourselves - our ability to be a sound, clear vessel to receive and transmit the Grace of God here and now.

Appendix

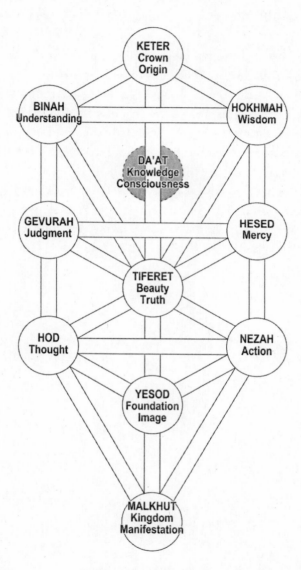

Fig. 1. The Tree of Life

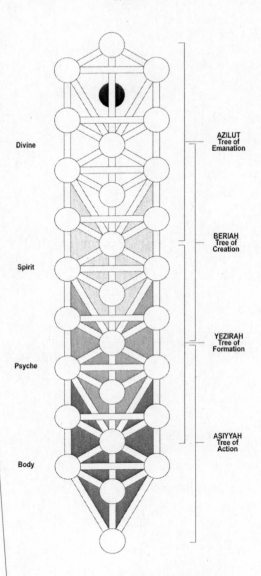

Divine

Spirit

Psyche

Body

AZILUT
Tree of
Emanation

BERIAH
Tree of
Creation

YEZIRAH
Tree of
Formation

ASIYYAH
Tree of
Action

Fig. 2 Jacob's Ladder

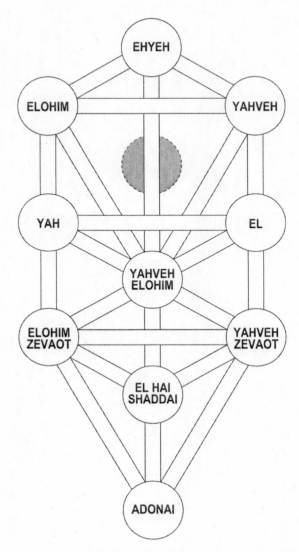

Fig 3. The Names of God

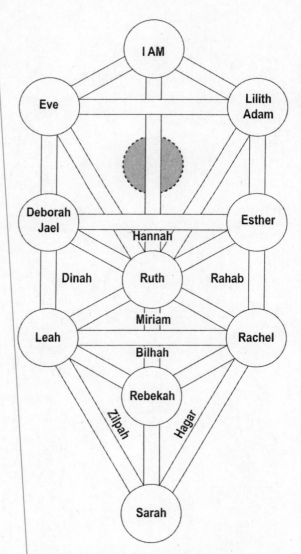

Fig 4. The Hebrew Women

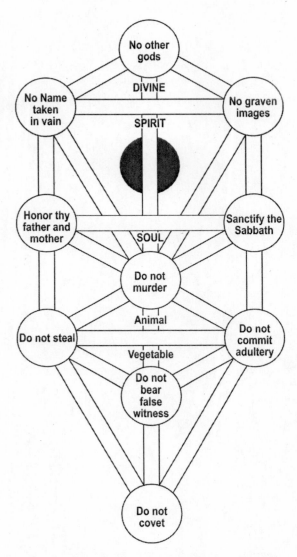

Fig 5. The Ten Commandments

Bibliography

The Book of Lilith by Barbara Koltov (Nicolas-Hays)

Hebrew Myths: The Book of Genesis by Robert Graves and Raphael Patai (New York: Doubleday)

The Hidden Tradition of the Kingdom of God, Margaret Barker (SPCK)

Temple Themes in Christian Worship, Margaret Barker (SPCK)

The Mother of the Lord, Volume 1: The Lady in the Temple, Margaret Barker (Bloomsbury T&T Clark)

Discovering Eve, Carol Meyers (Oxford University Press)

Households and Holiness, Carol Meyers (Oxford University Press)

Women and Religion in the First Christian Centuries, Deborah Sawyer (Routledge)

The Jewish Encyclopedia

Encyclopedia Judaica

The Absent Mother, edited by Alix Pirani (Mandala)

Kabbalah and Exodus, Z'ev ben Shimon Halevi (Kabbalah Society)

Kabbalah and Psychology, Z'ev ben Shimon Halevi (Kabbalah Society)

The Healing Past: Pharmaceuticals in the Biblical and Rabbinic World (Studies in Ancient Medicine), I. Jacob, W. Jacob (Brill)

The Masks of God, Volume III: Occidental Mythology, Joseph Campbell (Souvenir Press)

The Hero with a Thousand Faces, Joseph Campbell (Princeton University Press)

Patterns of Creation, Stephen Pope (Axis Mundi)

The New Oxford Annotated Bible with the Apocrypha, Herbert G. May and Bruce M. Metzger (Oxford University Press)

Major Trends in Jewish Mysticism, Gershom Scholem (Schocken Books)

Treatise on the Left Emanation, Rabbi Isaac ha-Kohen (public domain)

Tomer Devorah, Moses Cordovero (public domain)
Histories, Cornelius Tacitus (public domain)
Jewish Antiquities, Josephus (public domain)
Encyclopedia of Jewish Medical Ethics, Avraham Steinberg (Feldheim)
Websites: http://www.straightdope.com
Jewish Women's online Archive, particularly the work of Dr. Tamar Kadari, http://jwa.org

Endnotes

1. *The Mother of the Lord, Volume 1: The Lady in the Temple,* Margaret Barker (Bloomsbury T&T)

2. There are two extant written *Books of Raziel*: the *Sefer Ha-Razim,* a magical text discovered in the Cairo Geniza and said to be dated from the late third or early fourth century BCE, and *Sefer Raziel HaMalakh,* which can only be traced back to the thirteenth century but may contain significantly older text.

3. See *The Hidden Tradition of the Kingdom of God,* p. 26. Margaret Barker (SPCK).

4. For a fuller explanation of The Tree of Life and Jacob's Ladder, please see my book *Kabbalah Made Easy* (Axis Mundi).

5. See *The Seven Basic Plots: Why We Tell Stories,* Christopher Booker (Continuum).

6. *The Mother of the Lord, Volume 1: The Lady in the Temple,* Margaret Barker (Bloomsbury T&T Clark); citing *The Father of Joshua/Jesus,* S. Levin (SUNY Press); citing *Urschrift und Üebersetzungen de Bibel,* A. Geiger (Julius Hainauer); and *Les Tiqquné sopherim et la critique textuelle de l'Ancien Testament,* Supplements to *Vetus Testamentum IX.*

7. Irenaeus: *Against Heresies,* 3:11:8

8. *The Authorised Daily Prayer Book of the Hebrew Congregations of the British Empire,* translated by Rabbi S. Singer, revised under the direction of the late Dr. JH Hertz, Chief Rabbi (Eyre and Spottiswoode, Ltd). (I have changed words like "trusteth" to "trusts" for easier reading but made no other alterations.)

9. *The Roman Mother,* Suzanne Dixon (Routledge)

10. *Bereishit Rabba* 31:19

11. *Genesis Rabbah* 45:4

12. *Song of Songs Rabbah* 2:14
13. *Babylonian Talmud Bava Batra* 123a
14. *Women and Religion in the First Christian Centuries*, Deborah Sawyer (Routledge)
15. *The Healing Past: Pharmaceuticals in the Biblical and Rabbinic World (Studies in Ancient Medicine)*, I. Jacob, W. Jacob (Brill). For further details of the life and times of women in Biblical times, see my book *The Marriage of Jesus* (O-Books)
16. *Discovering Eve*, Carol Meyers (Oxford University Press). *The Mother of the Lord, Volume 1: The Lady in the Temple*, Margaret Barker (Bloomsbury T&T)
17. *The Masks of God, Volume III: Occidental Mythology*, Joseph Campbell (Souvenir Press)
18. *Patterns of Creation*, Stephen Pope (Axis Mundi)
19. *Mishnah Sukkah* 3.1–3
20. *Mishnah Aboda Zarah* 3.5–9
21. *Zohar, Conjugal Life* 147–187
22. *Zohar, Conjugal Life* 168
23. *The New Oxford Annotated Bible with the Apocrypha*, Herbert G. May and Bruce M. Metzger (Oxford University Press)
24. *Major Trends in Jewish Mysticism*, Gershom Scholem (Schocken Books)
25. *Treatise on the Left Emanation*, Rabbi Isaac ha-Kohen (13th century)
26. See my book *Prosperity Teachings of the Bible* (Axis Mundi)
27. *Genesis Rabbah* 8:1
28. *Genesis Rabbah* 17:2
29. *Numbers Rabbah* 19:22
30. *Christian Astrology*, William Lilly (Regulus Publishing Company Ltd)
31. *The Hero with a Thousand Faces*, Joseph Campbell (Princeton University Press)
32. *Genesis Rabbah* 41:2
33. *Genesis Rabbah* 45:4

34. *Genesis Rabbah* 48:20
35. *Pesikta de-Rav Kahana, Sos Asis*
36. *Pesikta Rabbati*
37. *Berachot* 40a and *Gittin* 62a
38. See also *Bereishit Rabba* 60:16
39. *Genesis Rabbah* 63:7–8
40. *Genesis Rabbah* 63:4
41. *Talmud Bava Batra* 123a
42. *Genesis Rabbah* 71:6
43. *Genesis Rabbati, Vayeze*
44. *Genesis Rabbah* 74:5
45. *Tanhuma, Vayeze* 12
46. *Genesis Rabbah* 74
47. *Kabbalah and Psychology*, Z'ev ben Shimon Halevi (Kabbalah Society)
48. *Talmud Sanhedrin* 102a
49. *Genesis Rabbah* 18:2
50. *Talmud Taanit* 9; *Targum Micha* 6:4
51. *Mekhilta de-Rabbi Simeon bar Yohai* 6; *Babylonian Talmud Sotah* 12a; *Pesikta Rabbati* 43
52. *Tanhuma, Zav* 13
53. *Talmud Bavli, Tractate Ta'anit* 9a
54. *Histories, Book Five*, Tacitus
55. Ezekiel 47:1, Revelation 21:2–6; 22:1, 17
56. *BT Megillah* 14b
57. *Numbers Rabbah* 8:9
58. See *The Last Temptation of Christ*, Nikos Kazantzakis (Simon & Schuster) and my *Book of Deborah* (Tree of Life Publishing).
59. *Ruth Rabbah* 2:1
60. *Midrash Eshet Hayil* 31:21
61. *Ruth Rabbah* 2:9
62. *Ruth Rabbah* 2:12
63. *Ruth Zuta* 2:3
64. *Ruth Rabbah* 4:4

65. *Ruth Rabbah* 7:10
66. *Ruth Zuta* 4:13
67. *Talmud Nazir* 23b. However, *Leviticus Rabbah* 23:10 attests that Jael did not take part in any sexual action with Sisera.
68. *Midrash Eshet Hayil* 31:19, *Batei Midrashot*, Volume 2
69. *Eliyahu Rabbah* 11:52
70. *Talmud Megillah* 14b
71. *The Mother of the Lord, Volume 1: The Lady in the Temple*, Margaret Barker (Bloomsbury T&T Clark)
72. *Kabbalah and Exodus*, Z'ev ben Shimon Halevi (Kabbalah Society)
73. *Yevamot* 6:6
74. *Pesikta Rabbati* 43
75. *Pesikta Rabbati* 43
76. *Pesikta Rabbati* loc. cit.
77. For a most human and elegantly plausible explanation for Esther's behavior and of her relationship with the king, see *Esther*, Norah Lofts (Tree of Life Publishing).
78. *Talmud Megillah* 13a
79. *Genesis Rabbah* 39:13
80. *Talmud Sanhedrin* 74b
81. *Talmud Megillah* 13ba
82. *Jewish Antiquities, Book 11, Chapter 6*, Josephus
83. Quotation from *Simple Abundance*, Sarah Ban Breathnach, Bantam.
84. *Maimonides, Mishnah Torah, Laws of Murder* 1:9; *Talmud Sanhedrin* 72b. *Encyclopedia of Jewish Medical Ethics*, Avraham Steinberg (Feldheim)